the Vörtex

TRAPPING AND EXPOSING LIES AND FALSEHOODS

VOLUME 1

by Michael Voris, S.T.B.

St. Michael's Media Publishing

For permission requests, write to:
St. Michael's Media Publishing
2840 Hilton Road
Ferndale, MI 48220

www.ChurchMilitant.com

Printed in the United States of America

ISBN 978-0-9989581-0-1 Hardcover Edition
ISBN 978-0-9989581-1-8 Softcover Edition

First Edition

for Julie

OTHER BOOKS BY MICHAEL VORIS:

Militant: Resurrecting Authentic Catholicism

The Weapon: Chaining the Gates of Hell with the Holy Rosary

CONTENTS

PROLOGUE

The title for the extremely popular *Vortex* came about almost through happenstance and in a somewhat comical manner.

Church Militant studios were established in 2006 in the small Detroit suburb of Ferndale just north of the city. Being geographically located in the more northern area of the United States and surrounded by the Great Lakes, the region is given to very cold winters and lots of clouds, even on warmer days.

The winter days seem to drag on for much longer than the three official months of winter, with only a few hours of daylight, and the whole scene can frequently be depressing and dreary. In addition to the dismal weather and sustained lack of sunlight, the original building the apostolate was leasing suffered from lack of windows. The few we had were small and narrow. Our working hours of eight o'clock in the morning until six o'clock in the evening (oftentimes later) did not allow for much exposure to daylight, with all its good effects on the brain and the disposition.

One day, a member of the original staff, Julie Komasara (now Muir), an outdoor girl given to backpacking and long walks, a true lover of nature, couldn't take the mood-damaging conditions any longer and shrieked from her office, "I can't take this anymore. I come into work, and it's dark. I leave work, and it's dark. There's no daylight that ever gets in this dungeon of an office. *It's like working in a vortex!*"

Thus was born the name of *The Vortex*. This event took place when the original staff was in the preproduction phase of the commentary piece, when we were casting about and spitballing for a name and could not come up with one. God sometimes provides in the least expected ways. As of the printing of this book, *The Vortex* has now been viewed more

than 30 million times and has become a staple in the households of tens of thousands of faithful Catholics.

FOREWORD

This is the introductory volume of what is hoped to be many volumes. *The Vortex* was launched on Monday, September 1, 2008, and since that date, more than 2,000 episodes have been produced, an average of about 250 per year.

The staff at St. Michael's Media decided there needed to be some daily presence in the Catholic internet world to provide a counterbalance to the daily pounding Catholics were taking from the paganized, secular culture. This was underlined for us by the wonderful, holy, and humorous Redemptorist priest, Fr. Pablo Straub, CssR (a regular on EWTN during the days when Mother Angelica was still in charge). He became great friends with us at the apostolate and appears in not only a couple of programs of his own at ChurchMilitant.com, but is also present at the opening of every episode of our flagship show, *The One True Faith.*

One day, during the early years, Fr. Pablo said to me, "We *need* to bring Christ to the internet." It was quite the challenge back then because, believe it or not, the internet was not yet capable of sustaining lengthy videos. The maximum play time on YouTube as recently as 2008 was only about ten minutes. This ruled out uploading *The One True Faith* onto that platform because each episode of the 112 episodes was roughly 50 minutes long, as they were originally produced and edited for commercial television broadcast. Thus was born the idea of a shorter form of video to "bring Christ to the internet."

Over the years and after thousands of scripts, various themes began emerging, themes that sometimes brought up issues the Establishment Church did not like or want being discussed. The attacks against the apostolate began in earnest, first from the archdiocese of Detroit, which began a whisper campaign against us once *The Vortex* started to take off in popularity. The archdiocese even planted operatives in the live studio audiences of *The One True Faith*—a fact we later learned from those in the chancery who were secretly friendly to our cause and agreed with our observations about the dismal state of affairs in the Church.

The first volume of this book and others to follow are compilations of scripts that actually aired and which follow along some of the more established themes and issues that have proven to be the most discussed and most viewed. Some scripts have been slightly modified for the sake of clarity and flow, but the substance remains in its integrity.

GOD love you.

INTRODUCTION

The Vortex has become one of the most recognized and perhaps most viewed Catholic video commentaries on the internet. With each daily episode being viewed an average of roughly 15,000 times, it has become the most consistently topical video in the Catholic world, paving the way for its home website, ChurchMilitant.com, becoming the most commented on Catholic website on the internet, coming in on average higher than number 300 out of millions of websites. No other Catholic website has drawn the number of comments and engagement that Church Militant has, with *The Vortex* leading the way.

The aim of *The Vortex* was to produce a daily commentary on the battle the Catholic Church has to undergo to catechize and evangelize in a rapidly changing social media landscape in a world often indifferent and even hostile to the gospel. Originally, the aim was to explore the difficulties and challenges the Church faced from the secular world. The first episode was seen on Labor Day, September 1, 2008, and was about Oprah Winfrey using her influence to push a New Age spirituality. It has to date almost 180,000 views.

The Vortex was originally set to air on January 1, 2009, but seeing how the 2008 U.S. presidential race between Barack Obama and John McCain was proceeding, plans were pulled ahead so there could be a Catholic voice on the internet warning about the threat to souls if Obama were elected. (It would turn out that 54 percent of Catholic voters eventually voted for Obama in 2008, and 51 percent in 2012.) So there exists a relationship of sorts between the ascendancy and reign of Obama and *The Vortex*. For the months leading up to the campaign, the tagline for the daily show was "Obama—soft on terrorists; tough on fetuses." It was our small Catholic contribution in the earliest days of St. Michael's Media to help focus Catholics' attention on the threat to the Faith coming from outside the Church.

Seven months later, in March of 2009, a most dramatic and terrible announcement came from the University of Notre Dame and the White House: President Barack Obama was to be the keynote speaker at the commencement ceremonies and would be honored with an honorary law degree. An avalanche of protests from faithful Catholics ensued, making their voices heard at the Catholic school. More than 300,000 joined in an online petition effort to disinvite Obama. I myself, a 1983 graduate of Notre Dame and a Catholic in good standing, had even brought forward a petition to the Holy See to appeal to the Church's code of canon law to prevent the appearance. That filing with Rome looked like it might still have a chance of working right up until Friday, May 15, 2009, when the weekend arrived and no word came from the Holy See.

In reaction to Obama's appearance and honorary doctorate in law, eighty-eight U.S. bishops protested (some by means of signing their names to joint statements from their state conferences, others individually). But counting the total number of bishops in the United States at the time, including auxiliary and retired bishops as well as ordinaries, there were close to 400 men consecrated as successors of the Apostles. Where were the protestations from those other 75 percent? It's a question we asked ourselves at St. Michael's Media studios in Detroit.

Obama at Notre Dame became a watershed moment for the apostolate in general as well as *The Vortex* in particular. The pathetic response by Catholics of all ranks to the Childkiller-in-Chief given honors at the leading Catholic university in the country revealed plainly for the world to see that the primary problem the Catholic Church faces is not from foes without, but from enemies within.

I was present at Notre Dame that fateful weekend and watched as Air Force One opened its landing gear as it passed over the famed Golden Dome, with the golden statue of the Mother of God high atop. I began to weep as I watched the plane fly over the campus on that sun-splashed morning, where a separate commencement ceremony was being held for roughly fifty graduating seniors (out of approximately 2,000 undergraduates) who wanted no part in the honors being awarded to Obama. That alternate ceremony was being held just in front of the Rockne Athletic Building on South Quad, the far opposite end of campus from where Obama was being praised and celebrated.

I was twice interviewed live on *Fox News* from the campus, where various national and international media had established their remote live feeds with satellite trucks. The whole world watched that day as Catholic identity was sacrificed for a celebration for Herod. On the three-hour car ride back to Detroit from South Bend, Indiana, the entire vision and aim of *The Vortex* changed. No longer would it concentrate on the evils outside the Church threatening souls. Its focus would shift to the evils inside the Church—evils that had precipitated the monumental collapse of moral order in the culture, highlighted by the travesty I had witnessed that day: the most pro-abortion president in American history being lauded and honored at the premier Catholic university in the United States.

Pope St. Pius V once said, "All the evils of the world are due to lukewarm Catholics." Observing the abysmal condition of the world the Church exists to save, it's easy enough to discern the condition of the Church Herself. I realized that momentous day it was time to begin looking inside the Church.

Chapter One

Glories of the Faith

REGARDLESS OF ALL THE MAYHEM, insanity, and theological lunacy that enjoy such prominence in the Church these days and has had a corrosive effect on society in general, two things must always be borne in mind.

First, none of this is happening without Our Blessed Lord's permission. However mysterious, and yes, perhaps even frustrating, the divine will may be at times, God is in control. This does not excuse those who still hold the Faith from confronting the situation, just as surely as it did not excuse the likes of St. Teresa of Avila or St. Ignatius from confronting the dire situation of their day—although the challenges today admittedly seem monumental compared to those of the past, owing largely to the world of media and communication that allow error and dissent to spread in an instant.

Second, always keep in mind the promise given to Simon Peter by Our Blessed Lord: The gates of Hell will not prevail. Hell will be unable to resist forever against the onslaught of the glory of the Faith, even when the attack against Hell has been seemingly reduced by earthly standards to little more than a whisper.

This Church, the One, Holy, Catholic, and Apostolic Church founded on Blessed Peter, is the repository of the Divine in all its fullness, Heaven on earth. Its teachings reveal the reality of existence, our destiny, and future glory. So fight, yes. Be aware of the ugliness of spiritual war, without a doubt. But, while bearing in mind those realities, always also hold in mind the glories of the Faith. The Church has buried every one of Her enemies.

From the Heart
Originally aired February 1, 2011

THE POET EMILY DICKINSON, contemplating her beloved, elegantly stammered a response to the question "How do I love thee?" vainly attempting to "count the ways," fully aware that such questions never have adequate answers.

What is the Catholic Church? Why do we so love and defend Her? Why do we produce episode after episode of *The Vortex*, exposing the "lies and falsehoods" of Her enemies, both within and without? Why are we so willing to fight and suffer for our Beloved?

The Catholic Church, the Bride of Christ, is magnificent. It stands, splendorous, like a great and noble city, a sparkling jewel. The Bride of Christ, loved from all eternity in the bosom of the Holy Trinity, presaged by Israel with the Father, purchased with the Blood of the Son, brought into visible reality and time by the Spirit, Her destiny is now eternity. What existed from all time in the mind of the Father will be alive forever in His heart, through the Son, by the power of the Holy Spirit.

The Catholic Church soars to the heavens in the depth of Her teachings, possesses infinity in a finite tabernacle, and glories, even now, with the saints and angels in Heaven as She lifts up Her heart in the eucharistic Sacrifice. The Bride of Christ, raised up from the dust of the earth through the waters of baptism, in perpetual virginity through Her everlasting espousal to Christ, lives and moves and has Her being in the Divine Majesty. She is the delight of the Lord of Lords, the Bride of the King of Kings. When She speaks, Her honeyed voice is truth and goodness and beauty. When She breathes, it is the air of the courts of Heaven, the intoxicating fragrance of love.

Our Blessed Lord would prepare nothing less than perfection for His Bride, just as He prepared nothing less than perfection for His Mother. The Catholic Church, the Bride of Christ, is worth fighting for. Her sons are summoned to defend Her honor, Her daughters to proclaim Her beauty. There is nothing more noble to which man can aspire than to sit in Her courts and muse on Her truth.

The deepest reality of love that God could offer to man, His very humanity and divinity in the form of bread, means that the very DNA of God Himself joins to our DNA, literally transforming us into Christ. The Catholic Church, the Bride of Christ, is one with Christ, Her Spouse. Through the reality of the Holy Eucharist, the very Blood of Christ flows through our veins. His Flesh becomes our flesh. We are prepared by slowly being transformed for our heavenly home.

The Catholic Church makes it possible for us to respond to the impossible command that Our Blessed Lord gave to each of us: "You, therefore, must be perfect, as your heavenly Father is perfect" (Matthew 5:48). When the Apostles heard such words from their Master, they were struck with awe and asked, "Then who can be saved?" Jesus answered, "With men it is impossible, but not with God; for all things are possible with God" (Mark 10:26–27).

The Catholic Church exists so that Almighty God may love us into eternity with Him.

So many people do not see the Church in this manner, a cause of continual sadness for those of us who do. It is what motivates and energizes us to pray and preach and sacrifice. The greatest gift this side of eternity has been handed to those baptized into the Catholic faith. Freely we have been given, now freely we must give.

The Catholic Church, the Bride of Christ, is the door to eternal life. She is wedded to Christ Himself as a wife is to her husband: The two have become one flesh, the same flesh (Genesis 2:24). When Our Lord says of Himself "I am the door" (John 10:9), He refers also to His One, Holy, Catholic, and Apostolic Church. He identifies with Her so closely and so freely that He made no distinction between the Church and Himself when he confronted Saul on the road to Damascus and said, "Saul, Saul, why do you persecute me?" (Acts 22:7).

One Lord, one faith, one baptism. It is all contained in the Catholic Church, fully and completely. This is Truth worth fighting for, the reason for everything that we do.

Catholic Dignity
Originally aired November 5, 2012

WHEN IT COMES TO MARTYRDOM of Catholics, it's almost always at the hands of the State. Yes, there have occasionally been cases in history of individuals or small groups that were not state-sponsored killing of Catholics, but those are exceptions.

Almost without fail, it is the State that brings to bear its power to try and crush the Church. Such has been the case throughout history, from Caesar on down to Elizabeth I of England to the French revolutionaries to Stalin to Mao Tse Tung and so forth. When we look at the French Revolution, much has been written and made about one particular set of martyrdoms involving the sixteen Carmelite nuns from Compiègne, north of Paris.

Their convent had been raided in August 1790 and all their property seized. The nuns were forced to leave their home and don lay clothes. Even as they scattered, they met secretly in community over the next few years, continuing their life of prayer together. In 1794, they were discovered, and most of the nuns were taken to prison on accusations of treason.

Unbeknownst to their persecutors, two years earlier, all the nuns had made an act of consecration to God, offering themselves as victims to satisfy God's justice. The prioress, Mother Teresa of St. Augustine, had proffered the idea.

"Having meditated much on this subject, I have thought of making an act of consecration by which the Community would offer itself as a sacrifice to appease the anger of God, so that the divine peace of His Dear Son would be brought into the world, returned to the Church and the state," she had said to them.

All the sisters, including two who were initially hesitant, agreed, and made the act of consecration. Two years later, God would accept their sacrifice.

The Carmelites were marched off to the guillotine on July 17, 1794, only a day after the Feast of Our Lady of Mt. Carmel, where they were each beheaded under the direction and orders of the Committee for Public Safety. As they were lined up for execution, they began to sing the beautiful Latin hymn *Veni Creator*, the same hymn they had sung as they took their vows years earlier.

Sister Constance, the youngest, was the first to die, then the lay sisters and externs, and so on, ending with the prioress, Mother Teresa—the very one who had proposed the act of consecration.

Unlike most public executions, which were loud, raucous affairs, witnesses say an eerie silence reigned throughout as the nuns were brought in the cart and marched up the scaffold, one by one. According to one eyewitness, the nuns looked radiant, as if it were their wedding day. Each knelt before the prioress and received her blessing before turning toward the guillotine, the instrument that would lead them to eternal glory.

Their bodies were dumped in a mass grave in Paris where more than a thousand other bodies were deposited, and as a result, first-class relics of the sisters have been impossible to positively identify.

Ten days later, Maximilien Robespierre, architect of the Reign of Terror, was executed on the exact same spot, bringing the French Revolution to an end.

The willing immolation of the Carmelite nuns had been accepted by Our Lord as a sacrifice pleasing to Him, along with that of thousands of Catholic martyrs who died for the Faith during the Revolution.

Their heroic witness stands as an enduring testament to us all.

Blessed Carmelite Martyrs of Compiègne, pray for us.

Christmas Sword
Originally aired December 23, 2013

C HRISTMAS IS ALWAYS A TIME to keep things in proper
focus, to put them in perspective.

That little Babe in the manger came to die. And to follow him
means violence. He Himself grows up and says, "[T]he
kingdom of heaven has suffered violence, and men of violence
take it by force" (Matthew 11:12). He's speaking of spiritual
violence, the ripping apart of ourselves, and putting whatever
evil there is in us to the sword.

The same Babe would also say in his adulthood, "Do not think
that I have come to bring peace on earth; I have not come to
bring peace, but a sword" (Matthew 10:34).

Following the Babe means violence, division, and hatred.
There is no escaping this. When light comes into a room, the
darkness is abused and driven out by the violence of
brilliance. Darkness is made homeless. And wherever the
Christ Child is, violence is right there, following like a shadow.

Within days after His birth, He is brought into the Temple,
and the old man Simeon unsheathes the sword for the Queen
of Heaven. *Because of Him, Mother, a sword your own soul shall
pierce.* Days later, the state pulls out its swords on the order of
Herod Antipas and brings forth the first martyrs of Christ—
the Holy Innocents.

Violence, hatred, swords—they are all over the pages of the
gospels. The Prince of Peace brings His peace through
violence and hatred, shown forth in the sword. Even on the
last pages of Sacred Scripture, as he comes to usher in the
final defeat of the enemy, he comes with a sword ushering
from His sacred mouth.

Ah, but these images never sit well with the Church of Nice
crowd. Too offensive, too unsettling, not . . . nice enough. It
will frighten the children.

"For this I was born, and for this I have come into the world, to bear witness to the truth," He will grow up and tell Pilate. "Every one who is of the truth hears my voice" (John 18:37). And those who don't will crucify Him.

The reason so many Church of Nice members, the country club Catholics, the emasculated clergy, will fawn and ooze and gush over the cribs and mangers near the front of the churches this time of year is because that's about their speed. They want a weak God, a cooing, slurpy baby of a God, lying there looking cute and cuddly, demanding absolutely nothing other than making goo goo faces.

But they are self-deluded. This newborn King demands your blood, your sacrifice, your sword be laid at the foot of that manger. You cannot love Him without hating the world and evil and sin. You cannot approach the sacred crèche without your sword drawn and ready to be placed in His service.

This is no mere baby. He is God with us, beginning His mission to announce the conquest, the trampling under and destruction of Hell—and anyone who loves Him must take up the sword and join in the battle until the day they die. To love God means to hate evil. The peace the Child ushers in is not a détente, an accord where good and bad strike some tentative accord, a pact of mutual non-aggression. His peace means total war.

"I will put enmities between thee and the woman, and thy seed and her seed: she shall crush thy head, and thou shalt lie in wait for her heel" (Genesis 3:15).*

The angels did not sing to the shepherds because a baby was born; they sang because His birth announced the final battle to crush underfoot their old companions whom they had cast out of the angelic realms.

Now, as the angelic trumpets blared and their voices filled the heavens with cries of *Gloria*, Satan and all his offspring were put on notice. The final battle was beginning, and he and his followers would be cast into the pool of everlasting fire. And there will be peace, and only then will men beat their swords into plowshares.

* Douay-Rheims translation

Roadblocks to Converting: Psychological
Originally aired March 19, 2014

THERE ARE THREE MAJOR AREAS where people offer objections about coming into the Church, and it's crucial to be able to identify which one is the person's main area of objection. It does no good to speak with them about objections to sexual morality if their actual objections revolve around how many books there are in the Bible. Practically every objection someone has can be lumped into one of these three categories: psychological, intellectual, or moral. And it's often the case that more than one category is involved in a person's objections to the Faith.

It's up to you, however, to identify which one is the predominant category and hone in on that. As the Holy Father has said, we need to be respectful of the person and try to understand him and his position. Just preaching at him does no good. But the point of the discussion is to bring him into the Church, not just win an argument or establish friendly chit chat.

With regard to the first category, the psychological, let's consider what types of objections might fall under this. This category deals with extremely personal issues for the person. He may have the personality type that's easily hurt, and past dealings with unkind or abusive Catholics may have left him with a bad taste in his mouth, as just one example. Whatever it might be, you have to ask questions, sometimes many questions, to try and get to the core issue, because the person himself may not even consciously know it. Maybe his father was abusive but also insisted on Mass attendance every week, and now in the person's psyche, Catholicism and his father's abusiveness are married, and the person feels rage toward both.

Or maybe his mother was dictatorial and controlling while also devout, and the person has now psychologically associated Church and mother together without knowing it. Perhaps a Catholic uncle who suffered from emotional illness was the role model for the person, and he has not, for whatever reason, unhitched his uncle's illness from the Faith.

You get the idea. Lots of people have many reasons for objecting to the Faith and not converting to it, or not returning to it. On a natural level, these people are hurting or suffering from some past pain. Perhaps they are holding on to it too long, perhaps they are unaware of it, but it makes no difference. The issue is that this emotional crutch is preventing them from seeing the beauty of the Church, and we have a duty to perform the works of mercy, to help ease their suffering in the here and now, as well as show them the truth, where they will find rest for their souls.

But this kind of work involves deep commitment on our parts. We must be willing to give up our time in order to speak with the person. We must be willing to give up our time in order to study the Faith and prepare ourselves to deal with these types of situations. As St. Paul said, "I have become all things to all men, that I might by all means save some" (1 Corinthians 9:22). It is love of souls that must motivate us and our dealings. Is it difficult? Certainly, because we all have our own baggage as well. But one does not have to be perfect to help others come to the Faith—just committed to the cause because we are committed to being holy.

It is God who brings about the conversion; we merely make ourselves available to be the tool He uses. And what a great blessing that is, to be used by Our Blessed Lord to draw a soul He loves infinitely to Himself! Dealing with psychological objections to the Faith requires a great desire to help the person. But it must be done. We don't get to leave anyone out from hearing the glory of the gospel preached in its absolute fullness. But as distinguished from moral or intellectual objections, psychological objections are their own animal and must be dealt with as such.

For example, some people may have personalities that don't like rules, that object to an imposition of morals because it makes them feel "oppressed." They see the Church as a great "Rule-Giver" and, consequently, don't want anything to do with it. You need to approach such a person and discover why that is the case and then help him understand the reality of the need for "rules." In such cases, the charge of duty is to help the person understand that the cause of his objection to the Faith is an insecurity or lack of a sense of self-worth, which he's projecting onto the Church.

Sometimes, some people are open to this view, and other times, their psychologies are wounded and it takes a long time to see this. What's important is that you keep trying as long as you can, as long as you see that it might bear fruit. No matter how frustrating it might be personally, the effort must be carried out.

Roadblocks to Converting: Intellectual
Originally aired March 20, 2014

IN THE PREVIOUS SEGMENT, we spoke about the psychological roadblocks to converting. Now let's turn to the intellectual. These can be all over the map. Atheists, for instance, won't listen to your Catholic drivel because they don't have any agreement with you from the very first point: the existence of God. There's no point arguing about the infallibility of the pope, or that the Church was granted this charism by God, when they don't even believe in God in the first place. These kinds of discussions must first be had over more philosophical issues than theological ones. The existence of God can be proven.

Then there are other objections of the intellectual category, including those that involve uncertainty as to God's existence, or the belief in some type of deity that doesn't comport with Christianity. This kind of person needs to be engaged in a discussion where the focus is on the inner nature of God, namely, the Holy Trinity, the inner life of God. Then there are, of course, the intellectual fissures in the various protestant groups, but even here, many distinctions need to be made.

The tens of thousands of competing protestant camps are all over the map with their understanding of Scripture, Christ, predestination, grace, morality, and a hundred other issues. You will find oftentimes that it's easier to talk with an unbeliever than with a committed protestant, because the unbeliever is being introduced to something new, while the committed protestant is much more resistant because he is emotionally invested in his faith, and to be presented with an intellectual argument that undoes most of what he has thought for years is simply too painful to bear.

Then there are those on the other end of the protestant spectrum who are perfectly willing to learn more and understand that there is much more to learn. The difference between the two is that one loves Our Blessed Lord more than he loves himself. This fact must be identified and pointed out in all charity.

Catholicism is all truth, and anything that departs from it even one iota is error. To the intellectually honest person, the Faith will appear to be exactly what it is by its very nature—Truth—and he will run to it. Your job in evangelizing is to locate these people (and they are everywhere) and spend the time needed to show them, as St. Paul might say, the "more excellent way" (1 Corinthians 12:31).

God has given them the flame of desire in their intellects to know Him, and He wants to use you to be the instrument to fan the flame. That means you need to have your intellect prepared. You must read, study, pray, listen, learn, in short, prepare to offer whatever part of your life you can to bring people to the truth. There is no intellectual objection to the Faith that cannot be addressed and resolved.

The Catholic Church possesses the fullness of the truth because Almighty God desires that all men be saved and, consequently, that they have access to the truth—and truth must first be apprehended by the intellect. Whether it's being able to explain certain teachings or Scripture passages or Catholic practices, it is our duty to do this for love of neighbor and love of God.

When an intellectual objection is brought before you by someone, answer it knowledgeably and charitably. Remove that roadblock so he can come closer to the truth. But the duty falls on you to be two things: both willing and able to respond. And that rests entirely in your hands.

Roadblocks to Converting: Moral
Originally aired March 21, 2014

W E'VE DISCUSSED PSYCHOLOGICAL and intellectual objections to the Faith. Now, on to the the most common: moral objections. It should come as little surprise that these most often revolve around sexual morality.

First, an important caution when talking to people about their objections to Catholicism: Frequently, people will say, or even believe themselves without realizing it, that their objections are from one category, when they're actually from another. For example, the daughter of a protestant minister may argue with you about the reason she would never consider converting to Catholicism because she thinks Catholics have it all wrong about Scripture.

All the while, the reality is that down deep, she believes converting would be a slap in the face to her father, and she doesn't want to hurt him. As we said, she may not even realize that herself and keeps arguing about intellectual issues like Scripture, when the heart of the matter isn't intellectual at all but emotional.

So, too, with moral objections. Down deep, many people know on some level that they are leading immoral lives. They may be in divorced and civilly remarried relationships, for example, or other sinful sexual relationships, like cohabitation or homosexual partnerships. (Notice that in just those three areas, we've touched on more than half of all Americans.) In such cases, you need to identify what the core objection is. There may be multiple objections, but one of them is the main one.

Other people with objections to the Faith in the moral realm are quite up front about that. They might, for instance, declare that they won't join, or stay in, a Church that won't accept homosexual relationships. Such was the case with movie actress Anne Hathaway. She and her entire family quit the Faith because her brother is an open homosexual and they didn't like the Church's teaching. She said publicly that it was meanspirited.

Others simply don't want to give up their contraception or unbridled sexual exploits. They know that to become Catholic and truly embrace the Faith would mean all that sin would have to come to an end. No doubt, these are hard nuts to crack. Many of them populate the pews in the parishes of the Church of Nice—not to mention, not a few pulpits. But it is precisely that they are so hard to break through that the effort must be made. Anyone who objects to converting to the Catholic faith, or coming back to it, is doing so on baseless grounds.

And the sinner who wants to hold onto his sin is in the most dangerous position of all. Mortal sin darkens the intellect; it keeps dimming the lights until they can go out completely. As Our Blessed Lord says, "If then the light in you is darkness, how great is the darkness!" (Matthew 6:23). And the countermand to that is Christ's charge to His faithful: "You are the light of the world" (Matthew 5:14).

The light must go into the darkness because the light conquers the darkness. The two are opposites, true, but they are not equal. Light is always superior to darkness. You will never see darkness extinguishing light, but you will always see light dispelling the darkness. Each of these three categories where people object to the Catholic faith—psychological, intellectual, moral—is a distinct kind of darkness, highlighted or propelled forward by one of the deadly sins: lust, pride, or anger.

We, who are tasked with evangelizing, cannot ourselves fall into the trap of succumbing to the deadly sin of sloth. We have a duty to educate ourselves in the Faith as much as we can. We must immerse ourselves in the devotional life of the Church, come to love the tradition of the Church, warmly embrace the Sacred Scriptures until they take us over. There is no way to do these things without committing to them. We cannot lament the large numbers of unbelievers who refuse to become Catholic when we ourselves haven't been willing to sacrifice far less in time and effort than we are asking of them. But we should lament the judgment that will befall us at our particular judgment before the throne of Our Blessed Lord.

"Go therefore and make disciples of all nations, baptizing them in the name of the Father and of the Son and of the Holy Spirit, teaching them to observe all that I have commanded you; and lo, I am with you always, to the close of the age" (Matthew 28:19–20).

It is our duty to help remove the roadblocks people have placed in their paths, regardless of which type, psychological, intellectual, or moral. We must identify the root objection they have and do whatever is necessary to burn it to the ground. Catholics in a state of grace possess the Divine Fire. It's time we started using it for the love of souls and the love of God.

The Reason for Church
Originally aired November 18, 2014

E VERY NOW AND THEN you get a little confirmation that
you are on the right track. Such a moment occurred when
I was speaking to a recently divorced, single mother of two
young daughters.

I asked her if she was Catholic, and she confessed she had
been, but said she'd had a bad experience in a parish when
they refused to let her daughters into First Communion
classes without her paying $400 she did not have. Her mother
ended up paying for them, but she eventually left and started
going to an Evangelical, no-name church, chock-full of former
Catholics, unsurprisingly.

Now here's where things became telling. I said to her that she
should ignore what happened and get back to the Church
because the one she was attending was a false religion and,
most importantly, they could not give her Our Blessed Lord in
Holy Communion.

She wasn't sure what I was talking about, so I asked her, "Why
did you enroll your daughters for their First Holy Communion
instruction?"

She answered, "Because that's what Catholics do."

I asked her if she knew what it all meant, and she confessed
almost total ignorance. She explained that her mother
believed all "that," but she was never interested. So I said, "Do
you want your daughters to go to Heaven? Why would you
take them to a Protestant gathering where they can't receive
the Body and Blood of Jesus?"

I opened up the Bible app on my phone and showed her John
6, explaining Our Lord's Bread of Life discourse. She became a
little fidgety when it came to the line "unless you eat the
flesh of the Son of man and drink his blood, you have no life
in you" (John 6:53). She then said the Catholic Church didn't
talk to her life issues. She said she "felt" better going to the

Protestant place because they talked to her about things she related to, like single motherhood and suffering and not having much money and so forth.

Then came the $64,000 question. I asked her, "Do they ever talk to you about getting to Heaven, about the supernatural things of life instead of just the natural things?"

Then came the answer that sums up everything: "I don't go to church to get to Heaven. I've never even thought about it."

If that doesn't sum up everything, nothing does.

Here's a former Catholic, almost completely uncatechized, who now attends a Protestant place that makes her feel good about her earthly condition and never speaks to her about getting to Heaven, which she is fine with because she has never given it a thought. She goes to the Protestant place because it's all about her feelings and earthly considerations. The truth is, she could come back to the Catholic Church and find pretty much the same thing in most parishes.

When I told her that everything she does should be geared to getting her to Heaven as well as her daughters, she responded slowly, "I've never heard that before or ever thought about it like that." And does anyone have to wonder for even one single moment why she has never heard this before? Because the Church of Nice rules supreme in the majority of Catholic parishes—that's why. Never talk about the supernatural when the mere natural has so much material to acquire diarrhea of the mouth while in the pulpit. Talk instead about the natural world and all its suffering and how we need to accompany people and think about how the Church can change its practices. For the love of God, never mention anything related to the supernatural. Way too controversial, way too unloving, way too not nice.

And here is the reality of never talking about Hell and preparing people for their end: Heaven and Hell are directly related; fail to tell the truth about one, and the other fades from people's minds as well.

Imagine going to "church" and never giving Heaven a thought. This lady goes because it makes her feel good because she hears about herself. All this oral diarrhea coming out of the 2014 Synod on the Family about accompanying people on their faith journey needs to be made much clearer. The Church exists to accompany people to Heaven and get them through life's suffering, to make the inevitable suffering redemptive and meritorious.

Why is there so little talk of *this* reality?

Things Visible and Invisible
Originally aired January 8, 2015

THERE ARE RULING PRINCIPLES of the universe. Why? How did the principles or laws that govern gravity, e.g., get established? If they randomly appeared, then why can't they just as randomly disappear and we begin to float?

It isn't gravity itself we are asking about, but the reality of the principles that produce the phenomenon of gravity. It's those principles we are asking about, not gravity itself. These are inquiries beyond the scope of the natural sciences. They can only be answered by the greater science, the meta-science of philosophy. But the philosophy must be rooted in truth and logic.

The celebrated and nearly worshipped philosophers of the so-called Enlightenment spent their lives developing a system of insufficient thought. Talk about a waste of a life. The modern-day heirs of their philosophical thought stumble around trying to provide an answer to the question of life. Natural scientists spend their time explaining the mechanism of life, the how. But that's a question more for the material world, things visible.

But before the "how" question is the "why" question. Why would life begin in the first place? What would be the purpose? What forces would lie behind whatever purpose? In the end, Catholicism provides truth and reasonability compared to modern philosophy or natural science. Catholicism isn't opposed to science, far from it.

But the Church is vehemently opposed to the misapplication of science, and for the record, when science is misapplied, it's not science anymore; it ceases to be science. Science means knowledge, and knowledge directly cor-responds to truth. When scientists step outside of the arena of truth and begin using the tools of their trade to wage war on truth, they cease to be scientists. When they, for example, use faulty philo-sophy to advance an anti-truth, they turn dark. And when you step back and apply a modern philosophical principle to the greater whole, it collapses.

As forces outside the Church try to make sense of the universe and man and society apart from the truth—Catholic truth—they greatly limit their range of answers. For example, for moderns, the existence of man *must* be a random event. We just evolved or appeared or developed or whatever method they desire to propose that cancels God out of the calculus.

Man operates according to certain rules and within certain boundaries. Where did the rules come from? What keeps them in place? How did the boundaries come about? What are the principles behind or undergirding the law that we cannot flap our arms and fly? Again, we're not asking about aerodynamics or gravity, but about the Law that governs the law of gravity or the Principles that govern the principles of aerodynamics.

Consider the concept of time. Why does it move in one direction? Why does it proceed at the same pace? Why do we see the same sky when we look up? Why is there not chaos as opposed to order? And on the even more invisible level, why is there love? Why do we cry? Why do we like music? In fact, why is there anything at all? There is no necessity for matter, after all, none the moderns have proposed, at any rate.

Matter must therefore be eternal for a modern, because it could not be conditional. If it were conditional, it would have to have an origin, and if it had an origin there would have to be a point at which it did not exist, a pre-existence of all matter, of all things visible. Since something cannot come from nothing, there would therefore have to be an immaterial set of forces to bring matter into existence. That is the only option for a modern free-thinker, the only option other than the belief that matter is eternal.

And allowing the very unscientific hypothesis that matter itself has always existed, that does not mean life has always existed. Where did the sentient originate? Better, why would it have originated? It's not necessary to have life to have matter. A rock doesn't have life. It has nothing more than existence. Yet even with a rock there are immaterial forces at work on it. Why doesn't it float? Why doesn't it crumble apart? Why doesn't it increase or decrease in mass? It has certain properties proper to it, but where did those properties come from, and why can't they change?

Something could not spring into existence from non-existence. What would prompt it? In the absence of existence, there would be by definition no governing principles because there would be no *thing* for the principles to act on or be drawn from. The immaterial rules the material, but moderns don't want to admit the immaterial.

And what's the point of all this? To note that there are moderns within the Church—modernists, who want the emphasis off God. They want a religion about man and the material order, about the visible world, because the invisible world scares the Hell out of them.

All of this is the direct result of the Protestant heresy. The logical end of Protestantism is ultimately annihilation of the invisible world, a universe where total subjectivity rules. It is why this heresy must be fought against so vehemently in all its forms in the Church—including men in the Catholic Church who are protestants under their robes.

Only the Brave Will Survive
Originally aired May 28, 2015

ONLY HEROIC CATHOLICS WILL SURVIVE. In short, in the times that are just ahead for Catholics, only the truly dedicated will not become apostates and thereby lose Heaven. This was the opinion of Fr. John Hardon, S.J., a very holy priest who died in 2000 in Detroit, a man who was remarkable owing to his holiness. What he said has come even more sharply into focus in light of the wholesale rejection of the Faith by an overwhelming majority of the Irish during its same-sex marriage referendum in May 2015.

If you are not preparing yourself and your family now, bracing yourselves spiritually for the darkness into which civilization is descending, you will not survive. You will inherit Satan for your father.

People do not suddenly decide to suffer for the Faith. They prepare themselves to suffer great hardships for the Faith by undergoing little hardships and sacrifices in advance. You could think of it as a kind of dress rehearsal. Our Blessed Lord Himself said conversely: "He who is faithful in a very little is faithful also in much; and he who is dishonest in a very little is dishonest also in much" (Luke 16:10).

Heroes do not miraculously appear. They have the stuff of heroism inside them all along, cultivated and molded and formed, waiting to emerge publicly if and when the correct circumstances arise. In the meantime, they live rather ordinary lives on the outside, perhaps even unaware them-selves of the reality that they are heroes in the making.

Such was the course of countless saints, who are, after all, the heroes of the Faith. But not one of them scaled the greater heights of holiness without first mastering the lesser heights. How did they do this? By choosing a life of prayer and sacrifice—prayer to unite themselves to Heaven while still on earth, and sacrifice to unite themselves to Christ suffering. Without the conscious choosing of this route, a person will fall away when the test comes.

We sometimes have this too-nostalgic thought about the age of martyrs in the early centuries. We see the drawings of heroic Catholics standing straight moments before the lions pounced. What we do not see, what is not memorialized in art, is the vast numbers who committed apostasy before the jaws of those same lions, or those in whom the Faith had turned cold. They were more than content to offer incense to the Roman gods.

And they didn't do it necessarily out of hate toward the Church; in all probability, it was just a mild indifference, just enough to get them to treat the Church officially in the same manner in which they had unofficially viewed Her. What the persecution did in them was simply concretize their ambivalence and lack of regard—a lack of regard that had come about long before they had lost their love of the truth, and circumstances just never prevailed upon them to make a formal announcement, something akin to the husband or wife who has long since stopped loving his spouse. He or she plods along, knowing the truth down deep, but not really having any driving reason to deal with it.

And then, suddenly, along comes the lover, the one who ultimately forces the spouse's hand, the one who makes the spouse choose; and he chooses to bring into the open what has been the reality all along. And he abandons the marriage. At last, circumstances did prevail upon him, and he chooses betrayal, adultery. This is exactly the same dynamic playing out across the Catholic world.

Many lackluster, indifferent Catholics feeling no real love of the Church will abandon Her as soon as the right conditions present themselves. Those conditions are arriving very soon—and very soon, the choice will have to be made. Only the most dedicated, heroic Catholics will choose correctly and be saved—and their number will be few. Pray and sacrifice that you and those you love will be among them.

We Win in the End
Originally aired July 8, 2015

IF YOU HAVEN'T NOTICED, there is a general feeling of
malaise going around the Catholic internet these days,
brought on and exacerbated by the U.S. Supreme Court's
tragic decision making sodomite "marriage" a constitutional
right. There is, however, something of a counterbalance to
the malaise also going around. It's the phrase "We know who
wins in the end," or its close companion: "We win in the end."

While that is true as it stands, it has the potential to inspire
many to non-action. It gives cover to those who don't really
want to do anything because they are paralyzed by fear, or
cowardice, or have just run out of gas.

Allow me to submit to you that this is a dangerous attitude. It
is also presumptuous. First, anything that excuses fear,
coddles exhaustion, or vents righteous anger away from its
justified target is bad. Second, it is presumptuous in that the
person saying it can potentially assume that *he* is included in
the "we" of "We win in the end."

Not so fast there. Our Lord and His Spotless Bride do win in
the end, have already won, in fact. But who is this "we" you
speak of? A person is only incorporated into the Church
Triumphant to the extent that he has been an active member
of *the* Church Militant. No Catholic can think the battle is just
some passing thing, not really affecting them, and they can
just wait for the reinforcements to come over the hill while
they essentially sit this one out.

We must, like the Enemy has done and still does, get up every
day and crawl out of bed every day with the mindset that
"today, you die." We must charge the gates of Hell and
overrun them. This means we *must* confront the evil and pay
the price for battling it. We need the attitude that we come
back looking like we have been in all-out war, and when asked
about our fight, answer back, "If you think I look beat up, you
should see the other guy."

All will be required to give their all, live a life that they never expected, sacrifice all kinds of things in the struggle, end relationships they never saw ending. This is a fight to the death, and this is the point too many—even faithful Catholics—are failing to grasp at this critical moment. Our Catholic lives must change—forever—because the world has changed—forever. And to the specific point: The world has changed forever because too few Catholics have changed forever.

It is insufficient to sit back and adopt the attitude of "We know how this ends; we win." It's almost a safe bet that many who take comfort in that saying will surely not be among the "we" they speak of. That "we" is reserved for those in *the* Church Militant who *earn* the privilege afforded by Heaven to join the ranks of the Church Triumphant.

We do know who wins in the end; we just need to make sure we are included in the "we."

The Church Is the Church
Originally aired October 24, 2015

I T MAY BE TIME FOR A LITTLE SHOT OF REALITY here.
There is much talk—evidence, actually—of deceit and
treachery from high ecclesiastics in Rome as well as from
other corners of the globe. Many have come to Rome,
Churchmen, with the idea of changing the Church. They
speak in words of mercy and all that, but their intent is to
dismantle the Church of Our Blessed Lord, His Holy Bride.
They want to not just put Her in different clothing so the
world will be more likely to accept Her and not be offended
by Her; they actually want to swap Her for a totally different
Bride.

This is what they want the world to perceive. This is the
message they want playing like a steady drumbeat in the back
of people's minds. This is why we have the never-ending talk
of new this and new that, renewal this and renewal that—new
approach, new listening, new language, new methods, new
ways, new everything. At least on this point, they're being
honest; they do want everything new. But their new is so
radically new that nothing of the old remains.

What we witnessed in Rome during the Synod on the Family
is the old guard's attempt to inflict a Vatican III on the
Church. They used and abused the process of the Synod to
bring up topics and matters for discussion that have no
business being discussed, especially at a Synod on the Family.
And likewise they squashed discussion on topics that *should*
be discussed, especially at a Synod on the Family.

A number of these wicked men see themselves as the
harbingers of a New Church to the world, a whole new way of
being Catholic—which, in fact, is not even recognizable as
Catholic, because it isn't. Under the clever cover of calling it
"mercy," they are willing to overlook and excuse the sins of
sodomy and adultery. To achieve that end they are willing to
add sacrilege to the mix in granting Holy Communion to
unrepentant sinners. Now they turn up the volume by

running wild with the idea of so-called decentralization, with many of them openly speaking about granting "powers" to local bishops' conferences, country by country, so morality and teaching can be determined by international borders.

A number of bishops we can tell you were shell-shocked, not able to believe their ears when they heard what is being said by more heterodox bishops in their ranks. Church Militant and many others, including clergy, have been saying for a while that the Church is in the midst of a deep crisis. There are quite a few issues to talk about in this regard, but one of the major areas of concern is, put simply, a lack of knowledge about the Faith on the part of clergy as well as laity.

Many seminarians and younger priests tell us with great frequency that they have had to learn the Faith kind of on their own. They stumbled across something on the internet, some piece of information or some story on a website like ChurchMilitant.com. They started doing their own research and investigation and began to understand on their own the depth of the crisis.

That's why sites like ChurchMilitant.com are so important. It's why we do what we do. We help bring to light, to expose the problems of the crisis so people will understand that they need to learn the Faith, to get into their heads that the Church is in one of Her darkest moments in history.

Catholics can no longer sit back and simply be content to think that all they need to know about the Faith they had learned by eighth grade. Look at the machinations at the Synod on the Family—the free-ranging, out-loud discussions by bishops claiming we need to handle sin based on borders and every other nutty idea you can imagine. We Catholics need to say *enough is enough*. The simple faithful are being rolled over by liberal, progressive, heterodox men and women in the Church who want to use the Church for their own designs. And they are able to get away with it because there are not enough Catholics who know the Faith to challenge them, to speak out against them, to throw down the gauntlet.

We've heard it said time and time again: Catholics don't know the Faith. They were not taught the Faith by these very men and their predecessors who wanted all this chaos to set in. When I returned to the faith of my childhood, I was shocked to see what I saw, and I grew up in the beginning stages of all this back in the 1970s. That's how this whole effort, this apostolate, began in 2006.

I resolved to do what I could to reverse all this, or at least to slow it down, and the resolve was oriented toward simply repeating the truths of the Faith, the beautiful teachings of the Magisterium. It's why I went and got a theologian's degree awarded from the Pontifical University of St. Thomas Aquinas in Rome. When it became clear to us that the reasons for such poor knowledge of the Faith was all this treachery by so many clerics, we incorporated news into our operation, reporting on stories, shedding light on and exposing their deeds and so forth.

But our original orientation has not changed. We are and always will be about helping others understand the Faith. Holy Mother Church has been betrayed by some of Her most trusted sons, and those of us who love Her must come to Her aid.

Make that commitment to learn the Faith, to keep it in front of you daily, studying, listening, not to the garbage from errant clergy, but to the voice of the Magisterium repeated through the electronic media faithful to the Church.

The Greatest Gift
Originally aired November 6, 2015

THE GREATEST GIFT HEAVEN COULD BESTOW on someone is the gift of the Catholic faith.

This is why we are so duty-bound as Catholics to ensure we are constantly doing what we can to bring people to the truth of the Church personally established by Almighty God. The Catholic Church is the One True Faith, and there is no other.

Yet in this contemporary climate of freemasonic principles of equality and liberty and fraternity, it is the most politically *incorrect* thing you can say—which is why it must be said even more, and with greater urgency. And to the point of this climate of theological poison that has engulfed the culture of the West, it must be admitted that the reason the Church is in such decline is because Her leaders have not resisted this evil of religious egalitarianism.

Either the Catholic Church is the Church directly established by God, or it is not. There is no politically correct fudging of that point. Is it, or is it not? If it is—which it *is*—then an entire reality falls from that single truth, including the truth that all other religions do not originate from Heaven, but rather from the faulty minds of sinful men.

In short, those religions, all of them, are false. Many Catholics today, especially leaders, just don't like talking in those terms. They make them uncomfortable, they put them in a position of being controversial and viewed as judgmental and not "nice" and all that hooey. This attitude, which in practical, on-the-ground terms translates into "all religions are pretty much the same," has to be eradicated from the Catholic mind.

At the moment, Catholic education and catechesis are saturated with this twisted understanding. It has zapped the life out of Catholic evangelization efforts. We as a Church have lost almost three complete generations of our own adherents because of this unwillingness to stand up and declare the truth that the Catholic faith is the only legitimate religion in the history of the human race. In the great push to be "welcoming" and "nice," we have frittered away our identity. This approach must be resisted.

The newest generation of children and young people are the Catholic Church's last great stand in the West. They must not be allowed to be infected with this spiritual poison. That's one of our main goals here at Church Militant—to reach out to younger Catholics and impress on them that the spiritual waters they are swimming in are polluted. And they have been polluted largely by our leaders, who still continue to allow the filth to flow in by not doing what needs to be done to prevent it.

A whole new approach—which is really the old approach—needs to be supported and advanced for home-schooling families, seminarians, young priests, Catholic college students. The tools we have at our disposal to do this are the internet and social media. They must be employed to announce the alternative message: the *truth* of Catholicism, not just half-truths presented in an unsteady, fearful manner. No saint was ever admitted into Heaven because he was trembling, nervous, and unsteady. They got into Heaven because they are heroes and lived heroic lives.

A few years ago I was talking to a somewhat high-ranking priest at the U.S. Conference of Catholic Bishops about an article he had written that was vague and ambiguous on this very point. So I called him, got into it with him, and said near the end, "Father, let's just cut to the chase. If you could push a button and the result would be that the whole world was Catholic, would you push the button?"

He hesitated—which was all I really needed to know—and then said, "No."

This lack of zeal, this lack of understanding—at the end of the day, really, this lack of *love* of the Faith has to be challenged and resisted. And it isn't going to happen by trying to convince the very perpetrators of the misdeeds of their errors and then waiting for a conversion. We are approaching zero hour for the Faith in the West, and we must rise to the challenge now.

Loving the Church
Originally aired April 26, 2016

C ATHOLICS HAVE ONE DUTY when it comes to Holy
Mother Church: to love Her with every ounce of our
beings, with a love that recognizes Her purity and desires that
everyone else recognize the same.

If you love your mother or wife because of their beauty, their
splendor as a woman, isn't it the case that you want everyone
else to see what you see? It's the same thing that motivates
grandparents to show anyone with a pulse pictures of their
grandchildren and get perfect strangers to confess that these
little tykes are the most wonderful in the world.

If this is so understandable on a natural level, shouldn't it be
even more the case on the supernatural level? Here is the
Bride of Christ, Our Mother. *Look!* Isn't She the most beautiful
thing you've ever seen?

Her Beauty blinds demons in their ugliness. And that's
because the source of Her beauty is the King of the universe.
Everything He is She is. It's why marriage is such a perfect
analogy. "Therefore a man leaves his father and his mother
and cleaves to his wife, and they become one flesh" (Genesis
2:24). Want to see Christ? Look at His Bride. He so associated
Himself with Her that He asked Saul on the road to Damascus
why Saul was persecuting *Him.* The fruit of the relationship,
so to speak, between Our Lord and His Church is *us.* It's why
we call the Church our Mother.

As we look out on the landscape of the current culture, we
must admit that a terrible scourge is coming for the Church.
We don't yet know the specifics, but Satan has been working
like mad behind the scenes setting the stage. From sexual
immorality, to the deadening of consciences, the dulling of
intellects, the overthrow of logic, the denial of any meaningful truth—this is going to break wide open on the Church.
If there were ever a time for such an event or series of events
to happen, the time is now.

In the nineteenth century, he went about his business in quiet, destabilizing a little bit here and there in the minds of various clergy. This continued into the twentieth century. It should be counted as no surprise that the Blessed Mother came with a warning to the children at Fatima at the beginning of the twentieth century. Before that century was over, a nearly worldwide rejection of the Faith—or at the very least massive confusion—would have been sown and accepted by the laity.

This great indifference on the part of baptized Catholics has been staggering. The diabolical has so whittled the number of faithful Catholics that he can soon bring war against them. But Our Blessed Lord has permitted this to happen. In the end, it will be He and His Bride Who will reign supreme.

Never forget the scene drawn for us in Sacred Scripture: Our Blessed Lord mounts His glorious throne and all the nations are assembled before Him. All of humanity is brought before this throne, and the Just Judge will pronounce judgment. This is going to happen. And it is only fitting that Christ will be the Judge in public before the whole human race.

The first injustice to be corrected will be the greatest. When Our Lord was last visibly present on earth, He was on a Cross, having been given the death sentence. The most innocent of our entire race executed—that injustice will be overturned first as all of humanity will behold His innocence.

And then comes we, humankind. We will see all the evil, the cumulative evil, of all human history. We will see what Our Lord beheld in His agony in the Garden. And in what will be the most awesome sight to behold, *the* victory that the Church Militant has fought for all ages, the Queen of Heaven will stand on and crush the head of the serpent, and St. Michael shall lay hold of him and cast him into the fiery furnace along with his demon legion, and then the human beings who would not pull free of his snares in this life will follow immediately behind into the everlasting fire prepared for the devil and his angels.

The elect will behold all of this. They will see with their own eyes, our own eyes, please God, what a miserable wretch Satan truly is. He will be the laughingstock of the nations; he who sought to climb the heights will be cast down, never to rise again.

And then the sound of victory will go up like an explosion. For our angels, this will all be a second act. They were eye-witnesses to his defeat before time, the actual players in it. The devil will have at last been utterly defeated, never to be thought of again. He will rule over Hell in the greatest of agony and never stop inflicting his pain and rage on those humans who succumbed to him.

But the glorious reception of the saints who will now be brought into Heaven with their glorified bodies has no words to describe it. All pains—physical, psychological, spiritual, all of it, every tear wiped away. No more death, sadness, nothing.

The Church Militant will have become the Church Tri-umphant. Imagine: We will be with Moses, David, Paul, Ignatius, Joseph, the Blessed Mother, assumed into the Blessed Trinity, world without end. We must keep our thoughts on the end game. *That* is the end game: salvation. This is why the preaching of the Church cannot be allowed to be blunted or compromised, ever.

The Church is pure. She is our Mother. She is Truth because He to Whom She is joined in eternal nuptials is Truth. She is the source of salvation because Almighty God wills that She be the source, so outside of Her there is no salvation. *This* is what we all fight for, a Church that has Her Master's power to raise the dead so that they may enter the Kingdom prepared for them from the foundation of the world.

Chapter Two

The Clergy Clash

F OR A TIME IN RECENT MEMORY, it looked like there was little hope for any rescue of the Church from the hands of heretical or dissident priests and bishops. Despite the presence of eventual saint Pope John Paul II on the throne of St. Peter, things seemed to go from bad to worse.

Little by little, the Judas crowd among the clergy seemed to be growing and extending its power and influence more and more within Church circles. From so-called social justice issues, to ignoring Church dogmas and doctrines, and a host of other "markers," including full-throated support for abuses in the liturgy and attacks against the Traditional Latin Mass, it appeared no Catholic was safe from the dissident crowd anywhere within the confines of the Church.

But a funny thing was happening on the way to oblivion. A few seminarians were being ordained who had kept their heads down during "formation" in seminary and were now slowly beginning to fill up the ranks of the priesthood. By comparison, they are still vastly outnumbered, but they own the future owing to their age and the suicidal track along which the aging Church of Nice is racing.

This chapter is helpful in demonstrating the contrast between despair and hope.

Saints Battling Saints
Originally aired May 12, 2015

IN THIS TIME when the Church of Nice rules supreme in the hearts and minds of many Catholics, all of them lukewarm, much of what has been understood in the past as Catholic thought, as the Catholic mind, the way of seeing things as Catholic—call it Catholic intuition—has been lost.

For example, in the great rush by the Church of Nice to accept anyone without question, without regarding anything they preach—the "All Are Welcome" nonsense—the Church of Nice has lost sight of the fact that Satan has disciples on this earth, in the here and now, at this very moment. And just as some of Our Blessed Lord's disciples in the here and now are truly heroic, living saints, so too, in a manner of speaking, does Satan have his "saints."

After all, what is a saint? In more traditional terms, when Catholics think of a saint, we think of an exceptionally holy person whose holiness is manifested by a superabundance of qualities like sacrifice, dedication, patience, tenacity, total commitment to the cause. Is anyone so naïve in the Church to think that Satan doesn't have among his followers people with such qualities? Of course, the goal of their dedication is not holiness but evil; but still, they are overflowing with these qualities.

The Ven. Abp. Fulton Sheen, whose track to sainthood is being deliberately stalled by New York's Cdl. Timothy Dolan, used to say of the Church's enemies, "They have all zeal and no truth, and we have all truth and no zeal." Take, for example, Hillary Clinton, in her attempt to be president of the United States. Is she not endowed with all of these qualities? She has suffered through the humiliation of an adulterous, skirt-chasing husband, subjected herself to public defeat by Obama when she was certain her time had come. She then submitted to further public humiliation by playing the game of party unity and becoming the Secretary of State beneath him. Of course, she used that position to elicit all kinds of money from foreign governments and entities to feather her nest for her presidential bid, using the Clinton Foundation as a kind of money-laundering set-up. She probably used her illegal e-mail set-up to conduct all this business, and then conveniently, the server that tracked all this melted down.

The point is the dedication she exhibited to the cause of seizing power. She endured humiliation after humiliation and never once took her eyes off the prize. If only there were more Catholics with her dedication. She was a power-hungry disciple of Satan back in the early years of Bill's presidency. While he was chasing "bimbos" (Hillary's words), she was already, more than twenty years previous, conducting her own panels and committees to change the nation's healthcare system. It didn't work, mostly because this power-hungry tyrant overstepped (she did all this as First Lady, not as an elected official).

In her first two campaign speeches since announcing her presidential bid in 2015, she declared her undying support for abortion *and* said that religions would have to change their teachings in this regard.

Hello, diabolical. We all know when she says "religions" what she really means: the being that controls her, who operates through her, intends the Catholic Church. Hillary is a "saint" of Satan. And she will do battle with the saints of Christ. She has already declared war on them. We can and should certainly pray for her—other satanic saints have flipped to the good before—but that doesn't mean we should not see reality for what it is. Satan has frequently used the power of the state as a weapon against the saints of Christ, not only in the United States, but even in Europe, as former Catholic country after former Catholic country falls in the face of the great diabolical sexual juggernaut.

Mind that you are not taken in by the appeals to human rights and justice and false mercy that have as their ends the excusing of sin. Sin excused or overlooked only increases the strength of the diabolical. Sin must in the first case be avoided and in the second case absolved. Anything else strengthens the hand of the devil.

Recognize the saints of Satan. Battle them and their hellish philosophies at every turn, and realize that not all of them are as prominent and obvious as people like Hillary Clinton. She is just a standard-bearer, but she has many allies just as dedicated and just as dangerous.

The Crisis Within the Crisis
Originally aired April 18, 2011

W HEN YOU LOOK UP THE DEFINITION for the word "crisis," you encounter two main thoughts: (1) a time of intense difficulty, trouble, danger, or instability; and (2) a time when a difficult or important decision must be made, e.g., "a crisis point of history."

When many good people look around the Church today, they see a crisis.

That crisis manifests itself in a large number of ways: liturgical abuses, heretical priests and bishops, Catholic faithful who really aren't that faithful. On that point, a poll exploring the issue of Catholics who practice contraception revealed that 97–98 percent reject Church teaching.

As many brilliant and saintly minds have expressed for centuries, when you reject one teaching, it's very likely you reject others as well. Most Catholics also don't go to Mass—80 percent, in fact—and most do not receive Our Eucharistic Lord, a fact that seems to check out when you consider that less than 30 percent believe in the Real Presence.

We've covered these issues and others extensively, trying to lay out why and how the crisis began. But there is one issue we have not spent a lot of time discussing, and that is why and how the crisis continues essentially unabated to this very hour.

The reason is that too many good Catholics simply do not see or do not *want* to see the crisis. This fact has created a crisis *within* the crisis. When one looks at the depth and breadth of the crisis in the Church, it's breathtaking. It's horrible and ugly to see. The Church has gone through other crisis periods before and always emerged stronger, but never without first accepting that *we are in a crisis.*

Often when Church leaders finally got around to facing the facts, much damage had already been done. For example,

Martin Luther was dismissed by Rome as little more than a drunk German. Luther had not been the first to foment a great revolt from inside the Church, but when he launched his revolt, something new had come into being: the printing press. All previous revolts had been largely localized because of their inability to spread far and wide owing to difficult travel conditions. Whenever a rebellion sprang up somewhere, the laity in other parts of the Church were by and large unaffected, at least directly.

But sociological and technological advances changed all that. Now revolution could be easily exported—and it was. Luther rocked the Church with his heresy, and the Church has never really recovered. It was a crisis, and when the crisis moment arrived and a choice had to be made, Church leaders whiffed.

Christianity has never been the same since. The Church lost a third of Europe.

Moving ahead to today, it is a fair statement to say that the extent of this current crisis is far greater than even the Protestant Revolt. Back then, it was a third of the Church that was severed; today, it is a far, far greater percentage.

Two things are different about today's crisis compared to Luther's Revolt, and one thing is eerily similar. First, the degree of heresy and its acceptance within the Church today differs from Luther's time. Today, it's a "soft" heresy, a quiet, almost indifferent dismissal of sacred teachings of the Church and a refusal on the part of many of those in charge to take any substantive action to kill the heresy.

Unlike Luther and John Calvin and the rest of the original band of heretics, there are no real firebrands, no fire-breathing detractors of the Faith. Today, they give speeches at conferences and write articles and appear on television interviews and are polite and buttoned down.

The second difference between today's crisis and Luther's involves the speed at which the revolt spreads. With the simple press of a button, one heterodox idea after another is foisted on the faithful in articles and emails. The use of the media by enemies of the Church has been masterful—and that goes for enemies inside and outside the Church—but especially those enemies within. Luther got kicked out and took his show on the road. These new Luthers stick around and kill from within. The damage that Luther did with the printing press looks laughable compared to the nuclear war that has been launched against the Church today.

Despite the differences between the Protestant crisis of the sixteenth century and the Modernist crisis of the twentieth, there is one major, scary similarity—and that is the unwillingness to face the fact of the current crisis. Some people are understandably afraid and paralyzed with fear, so they don't want to admit it. Others simply can't see it because they have personal dispositions, personalities, that cannot process conflict. They avoid it, oftentimes unconsciously. They cannot stomach the idea of the hand-to-hand combat required when a crisis hits.

The crisis of the sixteenth century took about fifty years for the Church to acknowledge and then another fifty years to begin seriously mounting a counter-revolution. That counter-revolution was possible in large part because small pockets of faithful men and women recognized the crisis and decided to seize the moment by forming new religious orders, preaching boldly to defend the Faith, committing themselves entirely to the defense of Holy Mother Church.

These men and women saw exactly what was going on and took action, often in the face of massive ridicule and mockery. They were able to perceive the crisis correctly and make the choice to march headlong into the fray, and through their efforts, many returned to the Church. The refusal by so many today to acknowledge the current crisis has become its own crisis within a crisis. We need the twenty-first century versions of the sixteenth-century saints.

Catholic Heritage
Originally aired February 16, 2016

THE PATRIMONY AND HERITAGE of the Catholic faith is flung to the far ends of the earth. At any given time or era, somewhere, future saints are busy at work, evangelizing, building, converting, preaching, and teaching. If you but peer into any moment in history, you will find such examples. On the 2016 Retreat at Sea, we looked into the 18th-century efforts of St. Junipero Serra and his missionary work in what is modern-day California. We visited the missions in Santa Barbara, San Francisco, and San Diego—San Diego being the first of twelve he established in the chain of twenty-one missions up and down the California coast.

It's somewhat difficult for us in the comforts of the twenty-first century to grasp the severe sacrifices these missionary saints made. But without sacrifice, it is nearly impossible to spread the Faith. Faith costs; it exacts a price from us—and this becomes almost instantly clear when you begin looking into the lives and works of any of the evangelizing or missionary saints.

For example, Fr. Serra traveled to Mexico from Spain when he was thirty-six years old. He had been a brilliant professor at Franciscan universities in Spain prior to this, but longed to convert pagans to the Faith. After arriving in modern-day Mexico, he set out on foot from Mexico City on the long and arduous Camino Real. A short way into the journey, his left leg developed intense swelling accompanied by an unbearable itch. It would often bleed and become raw, and this condition stayed with him for the rest of his life, every day, for thirty-five years.

He spent many difficult years in Mexico and then even more difficult times in Baja, California, working among native populations and building a mission there before he ever entered modern-day California. He established his first mission in San Diego in 1770, the first of what would become twelve he directly participated in and eventually twenty-one, from Monterrey/Carmel in the North to San Diego in the South.

Pope Francis canonized him in September 2015, the first canonization ever to happen on U.S. soil. Father Serra and his companions lived long stretches of deprivation of supplies, food, and shelter. Some of their mission work was attacked by natives. They were in conflict often with Spanish civil and military authorities in their mission territories, who wanted to conscript the newly converted Indian populations into near-slavery, which the saint opposed vehemently, even going so far as to return to Mexico City on his severely painful leg to appeal to officials to have one of the governors removed from office. It worked.

The point of this is simple: no pain, no gain. The Faith is not spread without sacrifice. Every saint in history is a living example of this. Here in the twenty-first century and in the West, we may not have to sacrifice in the body, certainly not in the same way, but we do have to sacrifice. We will lose friends, family, position, respect, and the like for the sake of the Faith. And the sacrifice must be daily.

A little-known fact about St. Junipero Serra was that, long before he set out for the so-called New World to convert pagans, back in Spain he was inflicting great pain on his body, mortifying his flesh, so much so that his fellow friars became worried he would harm himself permanently. For example, not only did he keep a sort of barbed-wire whip at his bedside to chase off sexual temptations in the middle of the night, he would also often preach holding a crucifix in one hand and a big stone in the other, which he would smash into his chest to inflict pain on himself in an effort to join in the physical sufferings of Our Lord.

Before he set off to convert pagans, he had already established the mastery of his own flesh and physical comfort. As a small point of reinforcement, during that long walk, once he landed in Mexico at Veracruz to Mexico City along the Camino Real, he had been offered a horse and he refused, clinging tenaciously to the rule of the time that Franciscans should never ride a horse unless it was a case of near-death.

We Catholics today live in a different era, and our living out of the Faith will by necessity take various forms. But the foundational principles of sacrifice and penance and suffering and loss are still the bedrock. The Faith cannot be spread without sacrifice. We need to sacrifice time to study and learn the Faith. We must sacrifice time to gain in the devotional life. We must sacrifice what comforts we can to promote the Faith, and we must be willing to lose earthly respect for the salvation of souls—even the souls inflicting emotional suffering on us.

There is no easy road to Heaven, and anyone who tells you there is is under the influence of the diabolical. A person must prepare intensely through sacrifice and prayer to engage in the work of the Gospel; we all must. This is a daily calling, and there is no easy or alternate path.

The theme of the 2016 Retreat at Sea, our fourth, was *resistance*—and this applies largely to ourselves. We must resist within ourselves all that drags us down in the work of evangelization. A serious look within needs to happen and probing questions asked, like "Why am I so concerned what others will think of me?" The love of earthly respect is one of today's foremost chains on Catholic souls, just as earthly comfort was a heavy chain on Catholics in St. Junipero Serra's day.

Yet as we look around today, it often appears there is no sacrifice too great for supporters of evil. Politicians and media under luciferian control will spend themselves to the point of exhaustion to spread their evil ideas. Professors, entertainers, lawyers, and various others will write, argue, publish, produce until they are nearly dead to infect the intellects of the masses—and yet most Catholics have no such zeal.

It's one reason we run the Retreat at Sea each year: to inspire attendees to become zealous for the Faith, to gather together for a week of intensity and then leave ready to do battle, to resist their own desires and indifference and then go out and help others resist their own. The Faith cannot be spread without personal pain and sacrifice. The followers of Lucifer know this and live it. They have learned to resist the call of Heaven; we need to learn to resist the call of Hell even more intensely than they. If we cannot look in the mirror and honestly point to big sacrifices we have made for the Kingdom, it's going to be pretty difficult to lay claim to it when we die.

The world is in the midst of great turmoil, and it needs committed Catholics, modern-day Fr. Serras, to undergo suffering for its salvation, for its evangelization.

Plotting Revolution
Originally aired October 28, 2014

I T IS BEYOND A DOUBT that what happened at the 2014 Synod on the Family in Rome was a trial balloon in an attempt to disregard Church teaching in the areas of the sacraments.

We say "disregard" as opposed to "change" because the revolutionaries don't want to be accused of trying to change doctrine. That would be too sensational and reveal their actual intentions. They have a multi-pronged strategy to get faithful Catholics to ignore the Church's teaching: They want to change the *conditions* in the Church, knowing they can never change the teaching itself.

Think of it like throwing a slip cover over an old chair that's been in the family for years. You can't get rid of it, but you don't have to look at it every day, either. That's what's going on, and it's dressed up with Church-speak: "keeping the doctrine, but changing the discipline." It's a clever ruse because many people wouldn't necessarily see the damage. It sounds "reasonable."

This anti-Catholic notion is coupled with another concept called "gradualism." Gradualism is the notion that people come to live a holy life step by step, gradually. But the end of the road is always clear: worthy and faithful reception of Holy Communion. In other words, from the beginning, a person is working on gradually overcoming his sin and sinful inclinations—the spiritual struggle.

That's what true gradualism is, and it's fine. It's what every faithful Catholic lives by; it's called practicing the Faith, and it's why the sacrament of confession exists.

Ah, but the revolutionaries have taken this concept and, while keeping the term, have changed the meaning. They—the unfaithful cardinals and bishops and other clergy—want people to misunderstand the concept. They want people to think gradualism refers to the slow acceptance of Church teaching. Note the difference.

Authentic gradualism refers to a sinner striving to be holy gradually. Fake gradualism refers to the slow acceptance of Church teaching, which means in reality that along the gradual road, various doctrines can be ignored and disciplines thrown overboard and disregarded because a person needs to come to accept them *slowly*. But see, that means that in the process of slowly coming to accept them, they are perfectly free to ignore them *until* they accept them. It's a giant smokescreen to allow people to use birth control, enjoy perverted sex, live together before marriage, all under the cover of slowly coming to accept the teachings.

Think about that for a moment. Let's say we applied that teaching to the secular world—to child molesters, for instance. The law would have to allow that child molesters need to gradually come to an understanding that society says molesting children is bad, but as the molesters are gradually coming to that realization, the discipline of throwing them in jail would be suspended so that they could continue in the practice as they gradually come to acceptance.

You can't run a society that way, and you cannot run a Church that way, especially when that Church has been commanded by the Son of God Who established it to teach all nations what He commanded. Now the more subtle, sneaky types will sit back breathless and offended when you point out that this is what they are doing. They will say, "No, we are attempting to accompany people on their journey."

When that sissy-sounding language comes out, avoid the temptation to punch the lights out of the person saying it. Instead, know that that language is the language of heresy, dressed up in syrupy, effeminate terms meant to make someone abandon the authentic practice of the Faith in favor of feelings. You are to walk with someone, "accompany" him by helping him become holy to get him to Heaven, not to avoid or refuse to accept his cross.

This is why so much of what went on at the 2014 synod is so revolting—the root word of "revolution"—because it refuses to acknowledge the supernatural virtues of faith, hope, and charity. So prepare yourselves to start hearing all kinds of talk about the "ideal"—which means Church teaching and discipline are proffered merely as an ideal, and not as an actuality to be lived out, and therefore we must approach all the supernatural stuff gradually—which at the end of the day means *never*.

The likes of Cdl. Donald Wuerl and many others pay lip service to the doctrine because they have to, but then talk about how that is an "ideal" and we need to rethink how we approach the discipline because we need to approach all this "gradually." All of these individual things are part of a larger whole, all ingredients in the big recipe to produce an overthrow of the Church, a giving in to the culture of the world, a willingness to alter an authentic Catholic approach and understanding in favor of a humanist one.

These are gigantic stakes, and the forces of the diabolical are refining their tactics after their mild setback at the synod. Be aware that you will begin to see and hear all sorts of things designed to undermine the Faith, but which will all sound very reasonable. And when you hear and see these things, remember what Our Blessed Lord said when His Apostles were stunned at the revelation of how hard it is to be saved (meaning how hard it is to get through the trials and crosses of this life and attain salvation): "With men this is impossible, but with God all things are possible" (Matthew 19:26).

Many leaders in the Church want revolution against God, to pursue an approach in shepherding according to man, and not according to God. Our Lord has already told them that pursuing this path will make their salvation impossible.

Think Like a Serial Killer
Originally aired November 24, 2014

THE FBI HAS AN ENTIRE BRANCH of skilled profes-
sionals dedicated to studying and examining the minds
and habits of serial killers so they can recognize them and
learn their thoughts in an effort to catch them and prevent
further murders. In short, these FBI specialists think like
serial killers.

If you want to understand the destruction of the Faith from
inside the Church, you have to think like a serial killer. If that
sounds a little over the top, consider this: Our Blessed Lord
Himself said, "And do not fear those who kill the body but
cannot kill the soul; rather fear him who can destroy both
soul and body in hell" (Matthew 10:28).

Satan is a destroyer, a killer of souls. And since he kills so
many, as Our Lady revealed at Fatima and myriads of saints
have revealed, following on Our Lord's own testimony that
many go to Hell, Satan can be correctly understood in terms
of a spiritual serial killer. And just so we are all on the same
page here, a spiritual serial killer is infinitely worse than an
earthly serial killer because the effects of spiritual death are
everlasting.

Now, we know that Satan has offspring because God Himself
tells us so when He curses the serpent. He specifically
mentions the offspring and says there will be hatred, enmity,
between the offspring of the Woman and them. Since Satan is
a spiritual assassin, so too then are his children. They have
inherited his genetic propensity for being serial killers. How
do you know who are spiritual serial killers? It's simple.
Again, Our Blessed Lord makes it very clear. He said quite
openly and directly, for example, to the Jewish leaders, "You
are of your father the devil, and your will is to do your
father's desires. He was a murderer from the beginning, and
has nothing to do with the truth, because there is no truth in
him. When he lies, he speaks according to his own nature, for
he is a liar and the father of lies" (John 8:44).

The connection is beyond obvious; it's blatant. Serial killers are the sons of Satan, devils, who do their father's will by deliberately lying and deliberately sowing confusion in opposition to Our Blessed Lord and His Holy Catholic Church. Whether they consciously kill and intend to murder spiritually is a non-issue. We aren't talking about their everlasting judgment, but rather the effect of their action and the reason for the effect.

Now, when we look inside the Church, especially among the ranks of the clergy continually agitating against the teachings of the Church, we see spiritual assassins, serial killers. Among many of them, the tactic is to speak in terms of not overthrowing doctrine per se, but rather to create an environment in which the doctrine is ignored or so marginalized that it's easy for the average Catholic to plug into this artificially created, evil environment and drink the poison. This garbage being spewed out, e.g., that divorced and remarried Catholics—those who are living in adultery, in a state of mortal sin—being able to receive the Body and Blood of Our Blessed Lord in Holy Communion is pure spiritual killing.

The game being played by those the pope has surrounded himself with is a game of false mercy, either pretending to believe or actually being so warped in their intellects to believe that the discipline or practice is so unrelated to the doctrine that you can still believe the doctrine yet act in a way that contradicts it. That is stupid, evil, and death dealing.

Consider how asinine it would be to think of a hypothetical doctrine in the family that your mother is queen of the house and deserves all your respect and honor and obedience, and then, for "pastoral" reasons, you could haul off and lay her out cold, and then go around and say, "We always respect the doctrine, it can't change, but sometimes, because we have to accept little Johnny where he is, and accompany him on his violence journey, we have to let him punch Mommy in the kisser until he comes to a fuller understanding."

It's such an idiotic principle—that how you treat the doctrine has nothing to do with what you believe about the doctrine—so moronic that it couldn't be applied in any other case in life. It's nothing short of a lie perpetrated by spiritual assassins who do the will of the Devil because they are his offspring. They are serial killers of the worst sort because they attack the children of God by laying bare the path for the diabolical to come and tear the sheep to pieces.

Pray for these men. Pray hard for them. It is beyond the capacity of the human mind to imagine what horrors wait for them in the next life if they do not repent. Studying serial killers and identifying them is a highly technical branch of psychology in temporal affairs. In the spiritual realm? Not so much.

Teach 'Em the Truth
Originally aired May 2, 2016

W E MIGHT BE SEEING A SMALL RESURGENCE in the Church in the United States when it comes to Catholic schools. There are many questions that will require time to be answered, but at this moment, there seems to be an admission on the part of some bishops that Catholic education needs to be shored up.

A place to start that effort would quite naturally be with the educators themselves. Since the demise of the religious teaching orders in the United States in the 1960s, huge numbers of laypeople have had to be hired to replace the sisters and brothers. That has caused problems, the most obvious one being that the cost of a Catholic education has shot through the roof. It costs a lot more money to pay lay staff than it does to keep a convent of nuns or a monastery of brothers around.

This has placed Catholic education largely out of financial reach for huge numbers of Catholic families. But the other and much more important cost has been the loss of the transmission of the Faith. Many Catholics, huge numbers of Catholics, even ones with good intentions, are at this point, after decades of horrible catechesis, simply unprepared to teach the Faith in anything beyond a superficial level. Not only are many of them lacking in knowledge, that lack of knowledge often spills over into their private lives and results in a failure to live the Faith. So we have a Catholic teacher population comprised of vast numbers of instructors who do not know or live the Faith in a truly substantive way. That spells d-i-s-a-s-t-e-r.

To try and remedy this, bishops around the country are taking a much more careful look at their teachers' contracts as they come up for renewal, which is generally every three years. In many instances, prior contracts contained loose or ambiguous language about teachers needing to live the Faith. The point may seem obvious, but it has certainly gotten short shrift. It's not reasonable to expect someone to be able to be a good teacher of the Faith if they aren't actually living the Faith.

You might say, "Well, of course." But this is the prevailing situation in many Catholic schools. In the case of Bp. Kevin Rhoades in the diocese of Fort Wayne-South Bend, Indiana, he took great steps to tighten language in his teacher's contract so every teacher and others understand that they may not live a life contrary to the Catholic faith and still expect to be allowed to be teachers.

Bravo for Bp. Rhoades. Talk about swimming against the stream.

The same central issue was addressed in 2015 by Abp. Salvatore Cordileone in San Francisco, when his Catholic teachers at four archdiocesan high schools wigged out about being required to actually believe and live the Faith they were supposedly teaching. A massive witch hunt-type PR machine went into high gear trying to discredit His Excellency, even taking out a full-page ad in the San Francisco paper asking Pope Francis to oust the archbishop. It was paid for by the usual suspects of deep-pocketed, liberal Democrats opposed to the Church's moral teaching in almost every area.

The role of Catholic education is not just to inform, but to *form*—to form students into holy, well-educated, thinking future men and women who can be instrumental in helping society stay centered on authentic values, and in the process merit Heaven. That has clearly not been the result of the last half-century of Catholic education, by and large.

Venerable Abp. Fulton Sheen warned back in the 1970s that sending your child to a Catholic school was an almost guaranteed way for them to lose the Faith. The problem has gotten so big that many Catholic parents around the world simply refuse and either home school, or support other Catholic education initiatives more inclined to safeguard the Faith of their children.

There are little glimmers here and there of a possible turnaround, but as of now, they are still small and largely fledgling. And this is true up and down the entire educational spectrum, from grade school and middle school to high school and universities. And it doesn't stop with just formal classroom education. The central problem remains in other spheres of education like RCIA and CCD and so on: too many people teaching who do not know or live the Faith.

That's why efforts like those of Bp. Rhoades and Abp. Cordileone must be supported and cheered on and prayed for to be safeguarded. Haggling over the language in a given diocesan teachers' contract isn't going to accomplish everything, not by a mile. But it is a beginning, a toehold in the battle to try and reclaim Catholic education, and frankly is the duty and responsibility of bishops, who are the supreme teachers in their diocese. They will have to give an account before the throne of Our Lord of what they did to safeguard these souls.

Pray for these bishops. Pray that others will also find their footing and take a clear stand for the truth in the face of massive criticism and bad PR. What matters is the truth and that it be communicated clearly. Be not afraid.

They Don't Believe
Originally aired January 19, 2015

I WAS TALKING to a young fellow recently and I asked him, "How would you describe the Church these days?"

His one-word answer said it all: confusing.

Everything is just so confused and unclear. He isn't old enough to have been alive at the close of the Second Vatican Council, but he nailed it correctly when he said that the things that happened after the Council, the way it was implemented, made everything very confusing.

True. But things don't just get implemented, as in they just passively happen. Things *are* implemented, and actively, by people with an agenda. Many clerics over the past fifty or so years lost the Faith, if they ever had it at all, and now they are busy implementing their agenda motivated by nonbelief. They don't seriously believe in the next life, certainly not in Hell, and by extension Heaven, or at least in the authentic understanding of Heaven, i.e., the infallible Magisterium of the Catholic Church. They don't believe one word of that. They don't believe in any substantive manner in the next life, so they have nothing to gain in the next life.

For them, this life is all there is. So their agenda of nonbelief and sowing confusion becomes for them all that there is in this life. It is truly for them a life-and-death issue. This makes them fully invested. This is why the anti-God crowd, both socially and theologically, are relentless, always pounding, never letting up with their agenda. No matter how many times they lose in the courts or see their agenda go down in flames when confronted by magisterial truths, they get up and come right back at it.

Oh, if faithful Catholics were only as determined as this lot. The homosexualist movement never takes a break, pounding night and day, non-stop, never resting. The crazy theological crowd, always publishing, always speaking to audiences, always blogging, always holding conferences. These anti-next life forces are fully invested in this life because they reject the next one.

So for them, climate change is a life-or-death issue. So too is illegal immigration, wealth redistribution, saving the whales, protecting Mother Earth. All these things are their substitute gods because these gods don't demand anything from them in the way of interior change. They can fornicate, cohabitate, masturbate, contracept, divorce and remarry, and sodomize one another, but as long as the white spotted owl is preserved from extinction, all is good. Kill as many human beings in the womb as you like, but make sure you keep a handle on your carbon footprint.

And in the strictly theological realm, keep the guitars strumming and those unconfessed Catholics cramming the aisles at Communion, and all is good. Just don't say a word about Hell, except to deny it, limit it, or create a nutty notion that no one really goes there. Call it what it is: a rejection of the supernatural and a replacing of the spiritual by the emotional. When Catholic clergy go along with this, they speed their way to the Hell they deny.

Sexual Schism
Originally aired January 30, 2015

A S THE BRILLIANT AND HOLY BISHOP Athanasius Schneider has observed, we are in the fourth great crisis of the Church. And brother, is this one unique.

The first crisis was over dogma, the Arian crisis, where the fourth-century priest Arius peddled his evil that Our Blessed Lord was not divine, was not God. The Council of Nicea took care of that . . . eventually.

Then there was the schism with the Eastern Churches, which certainly had a number of theological issues at the center of it, but also had involved a lot of secular politics, as the emperor kept asserting his authority over the bishops—and many of them caved in.

Then there was the Protestant Revolt, where, yet again, another cleric, another member of the ordained class (notice the pattern here), Fr. Martin Luther, again raised a fuss about dogma, denying it in essence and starting his own religion, which splintered to today's more than 40,000 Protestant denominations.

So about every roughly 500 years, a great crisis erupts in the Church, begun by a priest or bishop. And now here we are 500 years after the last crisis created by Martin Luther, and with this one still very much alive, another one hits. This one can be called the sexual schism, or the sexual heresy, and again, it has been brought about by bishops—bishops failing to do their job and, quite frankly, still even to this very moment, in the midst of the raging tempest, utterly and totally failing to do their job. And worse, too many of them are now not just staying silent in the face of the evil, but are actually signing up to help promote it.

This sexual schism is extremely unique in the history of the Church, at least on this grand a scale. There was the aberrant sexual weirdness of the Albigensian heretics, but these never became widespread and institutionalized like this sexual schism has become.

A couple of factors have occurred that contribute to this unprecedented spiritual meltdown. First, there's been a lack of zeal, a spiritual laziness, a slothful attitude toward the beauty of the Faith on the part of the laity, inspired by an equally slothful clergy. This began settling in in the late eighteenth century to the middle of the nineteenth century and became a kind of new normal. Catholicism, for many laity and clergy, was just like the furniture—taken for granted and overlooked. This went on for a number of generations and had the effect of softening up the Church Militant. We gave up our fight, put down our weapons, and went AWOL.

Sensing his moment, Satan began speeding events along, intuiting and observing a loss of faith, which of course is the natural result once the zeal for the Faith is lost. By the time the twentieth century dawned, all was prepared for a total overturning of sexual morality. Satan, of course, was able to launch his most direct attacks against the Protestant establishment, in this case the Church of England in 1930 when that body signed on to contraception, marking the first time in nearly 2,000 years that anyone who claimed Jesus Christ as God officially agreed to the evil of contraception.

Once that evil had been set loose, the Protestant denominations fell like flies, one by one all accepting it. Only the Catholic Church remained, so Satan set about not going after the doctrine (for even he knows that can never be changed because it is under the protection of the Holy Spirit). But the individual bishops and priests could be captured by him and wrapped around his claws and made to simply ignore the doctrine, refuse to teach the doctrine, sneer at the doctrine, openly rebel against the doctrine, and even laugh at the doctrine.

Contraception would come to be regarded by a large number of Catholic laity and clerics, either actively or passively, as no big deal. And in very little time, a sexual schism has been set loose. But it would not stop with contraception; it would advance to divorce, shattered homes, fatherless children, and now sodomy, with all its "gifts and qualities," as a number of bishops like to style it.

This is the time of the fourth great crisis in the Church, as Bp. Schneider has correctly called it. But this time—and this is what makes this crisis so perilous—the heretics haven't left the palace; they have seized control. At least Martin Luther had the common decency to denounce the Church and take his ball and go home. These modern scoundrels and heretics stay within the walls of the Church and in their robes, infecting the life blood.

They are the perpetrators of the newest crisis in the Church, not over dogma directly but over morality. They bow at the altar of dogma and pay it lip service while sharpening their daggers to kill it. These clerics, like their forebears of centuries earlier, have nothing but malice in their hearts and hatred toward the Bride of Christ. They must be resisted by faithful Catholics everywhere standing fast in the Faith. They have brought about the fourth great crisis in the Church. There will be much turmoil before this is all over. But in the end, they will lose.

Spiritual Criminals
Originally aired April 14, 2015

IN 1950s COMMUNIST POLAND, the Marxist leaders planned to build, in their words, "a city without God." The name of the city was Nowa Huta on the outskirts of Kraków and was to be a thoroughly modern city, with steel mills as its main production. The people revolted and demonstrated and clashed continually with communist police. As archbishop of Kraków, Karol Wojtłya was extremely successful in navigating a way through intense diplomatic channels to upset the communists' plans and get churches built.

Funny thing, though. At the same time on the western side of the Iron Curtain, a plan to get rid of churches and God was already being skillfully manipulated, and now it is coming to its completion. The old, hardline communists should have taken a lesson from traitorous Catholics in the West in how to destroy the Faith. No need for thug tactics. The Netherlands is a showcase example of what has gone so terribly wrong with the Church in the West, and it is being underlined and expressed by none other than the president of the episcopal conference of the Netherlands, Cdl. Willem Eijk.

He is the metropolitan of the see of Utrecht and is the seventieth successor of St. Willibrord, who established the Catholic faith in the Netherlands in the seventh century. This man, who is faithful to the Church, sent reverberations around Europe when it was reported by Vatican Radio's Polish site that Cdl. Eijk was proceeding with plans to close many of the Catholic churches in the Netherlands. According to reports, His Eminence said that because of mistakes made after Vatican II and the consequent lack of evangelization, the number of faithful has declined precipitously, and the churches are no longer needed.

In summary, because of traitorous clerics who became public since the 1960s, the Faith has been destroyed in the Netherlands. During Church Militant's time there, we met with a bishop and a number of priests, who all confirmed the state of affairs. Perhaps the most eye-opening, eye-popping thing we heard was this: There are 4,100,000 baptized Catholics in the Netherlands—about 25 percent of the country's total population. (It used to be 100 percent before the Protestant heresy took over.) Of the 4,100,000 Catholics, 4 million do not attend Mass. That's 98 percent of Dutch Catholics who have nothing to do with the Church. Of the 2 percent who do still attend, many are elderly, so even the future does not look bright by any earthly measure.

It should not be surprising that the Dutch Church would be hit this hard. It was the Dutch Church that produced the infamous Dutch Catechism. Almost more than any other publication, that book eradicated the faith of Dutch Catholics, as various bishops and clergy eventually embraced its errors and lack of clarity.

Today's bishops and clergy in Holland are reaping the poisonous fruits. Almost no one any longer believes the Faith. Those who do may be martyred. The closing of Catholic churches in Holland didn't just begin recently. It's been going on for quite a while—a dozen here, twenty or so there, some last year, others a few years back. It all began somewhat gradually and then picked up steam, until a trickle became a flood, and the flood became a tsunami.

The same thing is happening in America. The Dutch just had a head start. Unfaithful, cowardly, or naïve bishops have let the Faith evaporate. The pathetic efforts of diocesan evangelization teams and Establishment Church plans are proving fruitless because many of them aren't imbued with anything particularly Catholic. They are instead drowning in misguided efforts to reach out and dialogue instead of teaching the Faith. Our Blessed Lord commanded the Apostles to teach— not to dialogue.

So many leaders today are interested in being liked that the initiative is lost before it's begun. They somehow think that being cuddly and loveable and fuzzy will induce people to accept Catholic truth. You don't convince others to accept your theology by getting them to *like* you. That's Protestant through and through, where the appeal is a personal one, not an intellectual and spiritual one. It doesn't matter if people like you; what matters is that they accept the truth. And the truth when properly preached has an appeal of its own far beyond any passing appeal of the preacher.

The Catholic faith has been lost in Holland because the Faith itself was jettisoned by leaders in favor of appealing to the masses—exactly what Catholic leaders in the United States are doing.

The world has fallen deep into sin; it has come to accept horrible principles. This happened in past decades because Catholic leaders were spiritual criminals. The only way to bring some back from hurtling into Hell is to offer yourself up for martyrdom. Preach the truth, the Catholic faith in all its terrible glory, and whatever happens to you happens. But you can pretty much bet the farm you aren't going to be liked for it.

Preach the truth. Be martyred. Go to Heaven. Pretty straightforward.

Gay Priests
Originally aired July 29, 2015

A VIRTUAL PLAGUE OF GAY CLERGY and gay-friendly clergy has broken out in the Church these days. From the speaking circuit with priests like Fr. Timothy Radcliffe and Jesuit mouthpiece James Martin, the allies of the homosexual agenda seem to be an endless parade. One after another various priests even keep coming out—and where do these gay clergy come from? From seminaries that don't screen for them properly, or, even more worrisome, seminaries that actively recruit them, this plague of homosexual clergy has got to be put to an end.

We once produced a *Vortex* talking about a young fellow who left the Jesuit seminary life, not because he was straight and was revulsed by the open homosexuality, but because he was gay and was revulsed by the *closeted* homosexuality—or more precisely, the two-facedness of it all. He saw non-stop homosexuality in the seminary and order itself, and insisted they become much more public about it and give the gay rights movement a shot in the arm, a little support.

He said they didn't care. Why should they ruin a good thing they've got going? All the homosexual activity they could want and no price to pay for it. Fed up with the hypo-crisy, he left. At least he had the decency to leave.

But his story is multiplied many times over throughout the seminary system. All this talk about things are so very different than they were. "All that gay stuff was decades ago." That's what you hear. That's what the head-in-the-sand Catholic crowd say, the ones who can't stand to hear that things aren't nearly as rosy as they want them to be. The protector of the status quo, the apologists for the system, refuse to accept the idea that this nightmare of a scenario is real.

All over the country, gay priests have boyfriends (who are sometimes other priests) and are destroying the Faith in the hearts and minds of their parishes, classrooms, religious education classes, and so forth. They are pastors and professors and authors, and they are given a pass—a seemingly non-stop pass. As long as they don't commit a crime with teenaged boys, it seems anything else is allowed.

We here at Church Militant have personal knowledge of many cases like this, cases that get reported to us from parishioners and priests alike. The bishops know this is the case, many of them. We've had face-to-face discussions about the issue, and many of them simply don't know what to do. They are terrified of the repercussions of what would become an openly rebellious clergy. So they are convinced the best way to handle this is to do their best not to rock the boat and simply wait for the storm to pass.

But it isn't going to pass—or better said, it won't pass before most of the proverbial boat is destroyed. The Faith is being smashed away at, and this laissez-faire attitude is making things worse.

In one episode of *Mic'd Up*, we interviewed a former seminarian studying for the priesthood who offered a warning: Things haven't improved anywhere near as much as we are being told. He contacted us after our report about same-sex attraction in seminaries. He's married now with a lovely little girl.

This problem needs to be addressed much more seriously than it is. The seminary is no place for a young man to be working out his sexual identity issues. The problem is that there is a massive hold-over of clergy, many of them bishops, who were formed—or better said, malformed—by their seminaries that were ridiculously gay-friendly when they were young, impressionable seminarians.

Some of today's leaders are even compromised, unable to say anything lest their crowd call them out, like the former cardinal of Scotland Keith O'Brien, who said something truthful about the homosexual crowd, who then turned around and promptly outed *him*. Then there's the coming-out party where the pastor of Blackfen in England at a Traditional Latin Mass enclave came screaming out. And then there is former priest Bill Dickinson who wrote a screed about how the Church should uphold and support gay priests.

We could go on and on about this, but you get the point. How did all these homosexually self-identifying men get into their seminaries? And is anything being done to try and screen them out when they apply or help them leave once they are in, before they are ordained? Too many weak-minded individuals in the Church keep apologizing, making up excuses, and wanting to allow exceptions for this stuff. It's all born from a softness oozing from a leadership that never wants to hurt anybody's feelings and is willing to do practically anything to avoid it.

Are the seminaries doing everything they can to bring an end to this crisis? That's the question.

The CIA's Priest
Originally aired November 11, 2015

IN ONE VORTEX, we spoke briefly about the influence of Fr. John Courtney Murray on the Church in the 1950s and 1960s. While he is not a household name, don't let that deceive you.

First, he appeared on the cover of *TIME Magazine* in December 1960, so this priest was no lightweight. The big vexing question back then was: "Can Catholics also be good Americans?" The reason this question was so hotly debated was because of the understanding that there were things in the daily life of the country that Catholics could not square with their Catholicism.

In the 1950s, many of the more pressing questions we see now, like abortion, contraception, same-sex so-called marriage, had not yet emerged, but the potential for conflict was already foreseen by cultural elites and clergy like Fr. Murray. The cultural elites, like the Rockefellers, e.g., have a worldview in direct conflict with Catholic truth. The elites wanted to change the culture, turning it away from its Christian foundations, and were greatly concerned that the Catholic Church would pose an obstacle to their plans. The backdrop of the Cold War of the 1950s provided an unparallelled opportunity for them to move the needle.

Recall, this was the Cold War era: America vs. the Communist Soviet Union. The CIA was involved in all kinds of programs aimed at getting Americans to accept the general philosophical system of the United States as being good, if not the ideal, in all aspects of life: social, economic, political. So men like Henry Luce of *TIME Magazine*, with his close, private ties to the CIA, forged alliances with various religious men, most especially Fr. Murray, to help in this endeavor.

TIME Magazine became essentially a propaganda machine, a driving cultural force in this movement. And the relation-ship between Luce and Fr. Murray catapulted Fr. Murray onto the national stage. He became the waterboy for Team USA, the head cheerleader for All Things American. There were many Catholics opposed to his view, but they did not have the pulpit of the most prestigious, influential publication of the day backing them.

In buying into the "All Things American Are Good" proposition, Fr. Murray brought into the Catholic consciousness many things that were certainly American, but definitely not Catholic. This is why the question of "Could a Catholic also be a good American?" had to be brought up. At the end of the day, Murray and his crowd of CIA operatives and *TIME Magazine* won the day, helping American Catholics buy into the proposition of the separation of Church and State and calling it "religious liberty."

With the help of Fr. Murray, American Catholics became less Catholic and more American, to the point that today, in the time span of less than 60 years, people baptized as Catholics in America are indistinguishable from their Protestant or agnostic countrymen. In the great battle of allegiance to country or allegiance to state, the state won, backed by CIA operations aimed at achieving this very end. The Cold War merely served as a convenient excuse to convince American Catholics that country was more impor-tant than Church. It was the American Way that needed to win out over the Church.

And behind that multi-pronged CIA operation were the cultural elites, who controlled the U.S. government and its vast resources, who were able to use a priest to help seduce Catholics into accepting the American Dream in exchange for their faith. Popes had earlier warned that the notion of separation of Church and State was harmful and never to be accepted by Catholics as a legitimate political option. Looking at the results of its widespread acceptance by Catholics, now we know why the popes were so opposed.

Catholic, Inc.
Originally aired November 25, 2015

T HE RULING CLASS OF THE CHURCH continues to run the Church like a corporation. And we use the term "ruling class" intentionally, because there is something akin to class warfare going on.

And let's be clear here. We aren't talking about anything even closely related to dogma, doctrine, or teaching—that, of course, is the purview of the bishops, their obligation and duty before Almighty God. No, what we are talking about is this continual, persistent effort to treat many of the faithful as though they are peasants who should be dismissed out of hand when they raise concerns, objections, or even protests about the way business is conducted. And this superior attitude is not held by just some of the bishops and their staff, but also by those who hobnob with them. For these people, it's like a whole new kind of clericalism—the clericalism of the laity.

But it's the combination of both clericalist clerics and clericalist laymen that make up the ruling class, the ones who look down their noses at the peasantry. From Washington, D.C.'s Cdl. Donald Wuerl—who connives behind the backs of faithful clerics like Cdl. Raymond Burke to destroy those he considers his enemies because they actually accept the Faith instead of trying to demolish it—to others like Bill Donohue of the Catholic League, who has an extensive history of coming to the aid of any cleric no matter the wrongdoing.

Donohue *actually* said Catholics should *not* be talking about such cases as former archbishop of Milwaukee Rembert Weakland, whose homosexual affair got him blackmailed for a half million dollars before finally being exposed.

Then there are the Catholic bloggers who seem to have made careers out of defending and promoting Bp. Robert Barron and his undying support of the whackjob idea that we have a "reasonable hope" that all men are saved. Bishop Barron added to his growing litany of strange utterances when he gave an interview to EWTN saying the Catholic response to the Parisian ISIS terrorist attacks in 2015 should be one of non-violence.

Really? That's the solution offered with barely a perceptible hint of condemnation for the actual attacks themselves?

Cardinal Blase Cupich of Chicago dropped the bomb in 2015 that Catholics living in adultery should decide according to their conscience if they should approach for Holy Communion—and not a peep from Donahue or the Catholic League, because Cupich is ensconced as part of the ruling class.

There was a massive rally of teens in Indianapolis at Lucas Field where, gathering for catechesis and so forth, they were treated to more Event Catholicism, complete with the usual loud bands, light show, and appeal to all things "cool." They were even treated to a talk and video from former Catholic Relief Services head Carolyn Woo, who was traveling the country constantly painting a positive picture of CRS, despite its regular participation in Third-World contraception programs.

Now efforts are underway in various dioceses under the guise of the New Evangelization to marry together traditional Catholic beliefs and devotions, like eucharistic adoration, with jazzy, large-scale events incorporating bands, light shows, and lots of emotion—staples from the heretical world of Protestantism—one priest even going so far as to say we have the winning combination here: traditional Catholicism and Protestant expression of praise and worship.

Then there is the move in catechesis to the horrible program called Alpha, which many parishes and dioceses around the country have now woven into their Catholic educational material—nevermind that Alpha was developed by a non-Catholic who believes that all religions in general are the same, and that within Christianity, not much really separates Catholicism from those who follow the Protestant heresy. But of course he would believe that. The program is so theologically deficient that various dioceses and parishes actually had to develop a kind of Catholic appendix to it—so why are you using it to begin with?

On the social/political front, Catholic, Inc. has determined and instituted the policy of downtalking the "hard teachings" and playing up issues like illegal immigration—as in: If you express any concerns about Obama's open-door policy of accepting anyone into the country, then you are a "racist" and, worst of all, a bad Catholic because you are "mean and selfish."

And understand, my fellow Catholics, all of these things and many more are being orchestrated by the Establishment, the ruling class of the Church these days, who accept this nonsense as the new way of doing business: Try friendly approaches that don't upset people and play to the emotions; always play to the emotions. Catholic Inc.'s board of directors has determined that all of this will be the company policy moving forward.

If it sounds too Catholic, it is to be ignored, downplayed, or uprooted. Can't have too much overt Catholicism on display; people are put off, left feeling bad or uncomfortable, and we can *never* have that. It's all smiles around Catholic, Inc. these days, not to mention making a lot of money for the ruling class. Bill Donohue of the Catholic League collects almost half a million a year—almost $500,000. Carolyn Woo is in catch-up mode; poor thing only pulled down $400,000 a year as head of a Catholic non-profit. Who says you can't get rich fighting poverty?

Various other personalities well entrenched as members of the ruling class are cashing in as well. Even high-ranking prelates like D.C.'s Cdl. Donald Wuerl enjoy the high life. He lives in a top floor apartment in one of America's wealthiest neighborhoods, Embassy Row, as his supporters in left-leaning Catholic media circles keep the narrative going about how Wuerl's enemies live in luxury, without ever mentioning a word about the lifetime of luxurious living and jet-setting Wuerl maintains.

This is all bad enough, but what makes it even worse is that this Establishment, ruling-class approach to fixing things in the Church has failed spectacularly. As the Church somewhat lurched out of its out-and-out modernist approach to things, it didn't sway back to traditional beliefs with traditional expressions of those beliefs. Rather, Catholic, Inc. leaders devised what they thought would be a sure-fire strategy of cobbling together a little of this and a little of that—some Catholicism; some Protty, feel-good stuff; great, big corporate events to make attendees feel good about belonging to a much larger crowd; and so forth,

But you don't get to take pure Catholicism and mix in a little lack of piety, a spoonful or two of Catholic rock bands, a dash of laser lighting, and actually think you have come up with a successful strategy approved by the board of directors for rebranding the Faith so people will take a fresh look. The ruling class has failed; the Establishment effort has devastated the Faith down here where the peasants live—enormous salaries being collected while parishes are being closed; hip and cool rock-band Masses and 20,000-person events when the data keeps pouring in that Catholic youth care less and less about the Church.

Catholic, Inc. never ceases to paint a rosy picture of things. They have each gotten the memo, but the stupid strategy is failing, as all stupid strategies eventually do. And the reason is because the Church's main mission—to be the prophetic voice in the drama of salvation history—has been silenced and abandoned by direct decree from the ruling class.

Why is this the case? Because giant sums of government money can't be funneled to left-wing Catholic social justice programs if you are prophetic; because the fear is real that if you preach the reality of the day—that souls are being damned—that your donations will dry up. Donohue's Catholic League, e.g., is sitting atop an investment nest egg of $35,000,000 and has people wondering what exactly this branch of Catholic, Inc. *does* with that money—because each year it just grows and grows. They can't possibly be spending

$35,000,000 a year merely issuing press releases and blasting faithful Catholics who are sick and tired of the status quo.

The ruling class wants peasant Catholics to shut up and not protest or object to anything so they can continue to curry favor and maintain their seat at the proverbial table of power. They are so much smarter than all of us peasants. We don't understand the intricacies and nuances of dealing with civic leaders. We fail to appreciate the finer considerations of what would happen if the truth were just blurted out. Worldly respect; large financial portfolios; hobnobbing with powerful leaders and influencers—it's all so *above* us.

For all its sophistication and wisdom and groveling, Catholic, Inc. doesnt have one success to show for it. The Establishment does not convert anyone, but rather is converted by them. Slowly, bit by bit, one small surrender after small accommodation after another, they lose their Catholic identity—the Knights of Columbus national headquarters, the St. Patrick's Day Parade, and on and on.

Withdraw your stock from Catholic, Inc. as fast as you can, fellow Catholics. It's a sinkhole, a bad investment, and you may lose more than just your earthly fortune.

Do Your Job
Originally aired July 27, 2016

I T'S CLEAR FROM THE UPSIDE-DOWN, topsy-turvy world of politics that many are simply fed up; they've had it up to here. And what they are fed up with is what they rightfully consider institutional betrayal—a deep betrayal and treachery on the part of the various institutions in whom they've placed so much trust and confidence. To be betrayed by the very powers that you have ceded your own power to is heinous.

On the floor of the 2016 GOP Convention, Catholic radio host, author, and social commentator Laura Ingraham blasted the betrayal and those who perpetrate it. She first called out the corruption, the lies, the deceit, the treachery by those who have authority and abuse it. And then she went after those who are supposed to hold the cultural traitors accountable and will not.

We saw the vote by England to leave the EU. We saw the turmoil created even within the usually placid Party of Death, the Democrats, united as they are by their lust for blood and consequence-free sex and love of communism. None of the rank and file seemingly anywhere or in any organization are satisfied any longer.

Almost 70 percent of Americans feel the country is heading in the wrong direction. And the feeling of betrayal has skyrocketed among adherents of every stripe, view, and philosophy. Even for the bad guys, liberal political leaders, their former supporters have grown cold toward them, with, e.g., actor Matt Damon notably expressing his loss of confidence in Obama for his failure to be sufficiently liberal.

On every topic, on each side of every topic, positions are hardening and becoming concretized. The leaders of each side are being discounted and distrusted at staggering rates. With the race between Trump and Hillary, it's a virtual race to the bottom on the issue of trustworthiness and honesty. According to all the recent data, 57 percent of Americans deem Clinton untrustworthy, and 58 percent believe the same of Trump.

The decades-long miasma of scandal surrounding Hillary is astonishing, which helped fuel Bernie Sanders' near-upset of the queen of communism in what should have been a cakewalk for her. All of this distrust can be found among many Catholics as well regarding their own leaders, whether it's the bishop, the diocese, or the pastor.

Let's be clear here. Just as it's the case with politics, where there are largely two competing camps with polar opposite world views, so too in the Church. In America, there are 75–80 percent of Catholics who do not go to Mass, and roughly a fifth to a quarter who do. Those who do not go to Mass each week are not part of this discussion. In the world of politics they would be the people who just don't vote. But among voters (extending our analogy), among those who do go to Mass, there is deep dissatisfaction on the part of many.

Mass attendees are split between Church of Nice Catholics and authentic Catholics, and each crowd is mad at its leaders for differing reasons. Depending on which type of Catholic you are, the bishops are either overly conservative culture warriors because they don't proceed quickly enough with more liberal reforms, or among authentic Catholics, they are too weak and effeminate because they don't proceed with any degree of concern for asserting the traditional faith and tossing out the heretics and dissidents.

For the Church, this has boiled down to a betrayal of the Faith by various ranks of clergy for allowing the situation to reach this kind of impasse. Evil was allowed in, it has run wild, and the Church has been disemboweled, and only now are normal Catholics beginning to see this come into focus.

In the world of politics, the media are the watchdogs, as Laura Ingraham yelled at them to do their job regarding all the scandals that have rocked America on Obama's watch. In the Church, we have the unique situation where the leaders themselves—the hierarchy—are also the watchdogs.

As scandals of faith have buffeted the Church for the past fifty years, the faithful, authentic crowd of Catholics is crying out to the hierarchy: "Do your job."

Chapter Three

Crazy Theology

THE TERM "THEOLOGY" has a classical understanding, especially among seminarians: "Faith seeking understanding." But that has been turned on its head since the 1960s.

It seems as though the agenda of many in authority in the Church has been simply to confound the faithful and confuse the teachings with worldly pursuits; to regard the Church's teachings as old-fashioned and unwelcome, in major need of updating to suit the tastes and needs of modern man.

The motives for these actions by these men (and by women religious, who exercise much influence) are as varied as the leaders who pursue or allow all this, but the effect is, nonetheless, the same: a crazy theology that has little to do with the nineteen preceding centuries of theology.

Modern catechisms and religious education classes and materials have proven themselves near-failures in attempting to educate and form Catholics. In fact, it could easily be argued they have actually deformed Catholics, meaning it would have been better had they received no instruction in the Faith than poor instruction in crazy theology.

Pope Benedict, while he was still Cdl. Joseph Ratzinger, surveyed the whole dilemma from high atop his position as prefect of the Congregation for the Doctrine of the Faith, and concluded that the Church was going to have to survive a period of malformed clerics and bishops. The question now emerging is: Can the Church recover from the crazy theology that's become stock and trade in many quarters and the death spiral be reversed?

Catholic Tribes
Originally aired November 7, 2014

THERE IS A RIDICULOUS NOTION beginning to establish itself in Catholic circles that needs the big smack-down treatment. It's this notion circulating in blogs and articles about there being Catholic "tribes"—meaning different camps within the Church at odds with one another, oftentimes over questions of doctrine.

The idea may have first been voiced by Catholic journalist John Allen, who used to report for the dissident newspaper *National Catholic Reporter* (which has rightfully earned the nickname *National Catholic Distorter*). The paper was ordered by its bishop back in the 1960s to stop using the name "Catholic"—and it told him to go fly an ecclesiastical kite.

John Allen went on to write for an arm of the purely secular newspaper the *Boston Globe* for the website *Crux*. While his actual reporting of events is generally spot on and informative, he writes from a perspective that at best can be described as "questionable" when it comes to being faithful to the Church. This notion of "tribes" is one such example. He correctly reports that there are various camps of baptized Catholics vying for their own agendas—the tribes.

Some, he notes, are in favor of women's ordination, others lobby for same-sex "marriage," or divorced and civilly remarried Catholics being admitted to Holy Communion, and so forth. That's all true enough. But the distinction that Allen fails to make, either because he doesn't understand it or chooses to ignore it, is this: Baptized Catholics challenging Church dogma have placed themselves outside the Church.

In his reporting, Allen treats faithful Catholics and unfaithful Catholics as all being equal voices in the Church. They are not. He fails spectacularly to differentiate between living and dead members of the body of Christ. Granted, this moves in to the area of theology, and Allen does not hold himself out as a theologian or apologist for the Faith. Fair enough. But as a reporter, a journalist, it is incumbent on him to report the facts of the case completely. And the complete truth is that baptized Catholics who reject Church teaching are dead members of the body of Christ and therefore do not enjoy the right to be considered a legitimate voice in the Church, equal to faithful voices.

We have an omnipotent God Who has the power to raise the dead, and our 2,000-year sacred history is bursting at the seams with such examples. We should pray for and actively work toward the conversion (the resurrection, if you will) of the dead members. But until that occurs, they remain spiritual corpses. It is wrong reporting and horrible theology not to know or make that distinction.

Catholics owe Church teaching assent of the intellect, meaning that if the Church has defined something and a person disagrees, they are duty-bound in their Catholicism to accept that they are wrong, and they need to go back and figure out where they messed up. Allen ignores or glosses over this fundamental aspect and, consequently, it calls into question the integrity of his reports. It demonstrates an insufficient understanding or willingness to admit a foundational reality: Catholics who actively reject Church teaching have brought about their own spiritual death.

As Our Blessed Lord said to the Apostles, "He who hears you hears me, and he who rejects you rejects me, and he who rejects me rejects him who sent me" (Luke 10:16). It is journalistically disingenuous to present people as viable Catholics who by their own actions have removed themselves from that category. The problem is that a reader who reads stories written in this vein can walk away with the idea that dissent from magisterial teaching is a legitimate option; dissent is just "another" approach. But a person who was baptized a Catholic and who supports sodomy, e.g., certainly retains his baptism, but he no longer holds the Faith. As St. Paul instructs Timothy regarding some who had previously been baptized, "By rejecting conscience, certain persons have made shipwreck of their faith" (1 Timothy 1:19).

Imagine for a moment that a group of former Republicans who are now Democrats showed up at the Republican National Convention saying the GOP is wrong about a list of things. How journalistically sound would it be for reporters to file stories and say that a group of "Republicans" is challenging a host of Republican policies, without mentioning that they are no longer Republicans? This idiotic idea that there are legitimate voices within the Church that disparage Church teaching needs to be confronted and beaten down.

A Catholic accepts, no, more than accepts—holds dear to his heart—all the teachings of the Church. He embraces them, lives by them, loves them with his entire being. A Catholic who rejects them isn't alive in his faith; he is dead. He should not approach for Holy Communion, he should not spread his errors and pass them off as legitimate Catholic positions. And he certainly shouldn't be treated by journalists as though what he says is representative of a line of thought in the Church. It may be a line of thought, but it isn't *in* the Church.

"At Least They're Coming"
Originally aired January 5, 2015

WHEN YOU UNDERSTAND THE REAL MEANING of Christmas, not the sappy, syrupy, un-supernatural one that Pope Francis condemned and too many Catholic clerics swear by, you aren't capable of having any other reaction than being completely turned off by the neo-modernist, Church of Nice party line by priests and bishops who say of the Christmas and Easter Catholics, "Well, at least they're coming."

How patently stupid and absurd can you be? It demonstrates a complete lack of a Catholic mind and attitude toward the greatest crisis in the Church in centuries, perhaps ever. But it has become the only response the Church of Nice can muster because, having long ago jettisoned truth in favor of emotions, they have their ever-shrinking crowds trained to look for emotional highs and not truth.

News flash to the Church of Nice hierarchy and its fan base: The world has much more to offer in the way of temporal, emotional highs than the Church could even imagine. Appearing on Fox News to talk about the NYPD murders, Cdl. Timothy Dolan didn't take long to get into the Church of Nice monologue of "at least they're here" in reference to a question asked him about the Christmas and Easter crowd of Catholics. In his words, "I'm thrilled they're here for Christmas and Easter. Alleluia. Come on in. We're glad you're here. Let's pray. Hope you enjoy it. We're doing the same thing on Sunday. Come on back."

This is beyond pathetic. But it is the greeting on the Christmas cards mailed out by the Church of Nice. All over the country, for years now, this is the line that comes spewing out of the mouths of clerics on Christmas Day. "Welcome! We do this every Sunday as well." Everyone gives a polite chuckle, and that's the last appeal to truth, to their conscience, they will hear. Forget about all that talk of Jesus the Savior. Forget about the cost of martyrdom it takes to approach this crib or hold this Infant. Just focus on the sappy emotions and sing songs that might stir those emotions for a couple of minutes, but then watch the lines of hundreds of people coming up to commit sacrilege by unworthy reception of the Body and Blood of the Savior. Right, Happy Birthday, Jesus. From the Church of Nice!

The very reason God became an Infant, the only reason—to save us from Hell—these clerics undermine by failing to say plainly. They express the inauthentic Catholic faith because they express an incomplete Catholic faith; and an incomplete Catholic faith is called the Protestant heresy. These leaders of inauthentic Catholicism leave countless Catholics in their sin, never telling them to get back to confession. They refuse to inform them that to come up and receive Holy Communion if they haven't gone to Mass or confession is a sacrilege and adds to their guilt. Never tell them the real meaning of Christmas; the real reason Almighty God had to so humble Himself: to save them from Hell.

Christmas is not about emotions, even though it of course evokes an emotional response. It is solely about God entering time to save us from Satan. And that is all it is about. Christmas is merely the celebration of that plan finally becoming visible to the eye. As for the sissy-speak line "We're glad you're here"—are we? Really? Should we be? Because many of us are here for a totally different reason. Many of us are here to worship God; others are here to worship their own feelings and feed their own season-inspired nostalgia, nothing more.

Remember the scene the day after Our Blessed Lord performed the miracle of the loaves and fed the thousands. Those thousands tracked Him down in Capernaum. And what did Almighty God do? He called them out on their hypocrisy. Invoking His Divinity, he thundered, "Truly, truly, I say to you,

you seek me, not because you saw signs, but because you ate your fill of the loaves" (John 6:26).

And that's what this emasculated group of bishops and clerics refuses to face: that the hordes of people sitting in front of them at Midnight Mass or Christmas Day Mass are not there because they believe but because they want their fill of nostalgia. They are there for the bread that perishes, not the Bread that gives life eternal. And if that damning truth rings too harshly in the ears of the Church of Nice pantywaists, then ask yourselves this burning question: If your "nice" approach works so well and hiding or ignoring the truth is the best way to go, then why in the New York archdiocese have you closed down almost a hundred parishes in the last ten years?

We know the answer to that: because your highly charged, hyperfeminized approach doesn't work, because it cannot work, because it is doomed to failure right out of the gate. It denies the truth, obscures the truth, refuses to say the whole truth. Either these leaders don't believe the fullness of Catholicism, or they are too afraid to announce it; in either case you do the work of Satan by starving the sheep. You and your lot certainly aren't like those first shepherds to behold the Christ Child, whose recounting of the real meaning of all this the Mother of God pondered and treasured in Her Immaculate Heart. What precisely would the Queen of Heaven be pondering over with your sappy pandering to the masses?

And Cdl. Dolan certainly isn't alone in this; he just keeps making himself the visible spokesman for the Church of Nice sputum. He represents a whole gaggle of bishops who were malformed in the seminaries of the 1960s and 1970s. Their inauthentic Catholicism emphasizes the natural, not the supernatural. And they will be held to account for it, every last one of them, because of the number of souls they have deprived of the truth. These men should be quaking in their boots. They only have a few years, if that, before they go to God.

Christmas and Easter Catholics may have some small ember of faith, but you do nothing to fan it into the raging fire God desires it to be. You show them no beauty. You're content to play to their emotions while ignoring their intellects. You do not care about their souls, but only getting their bodies in the pews. That's why they don't come back on the following Sunday, skip the Holy Day of Obligation on January 1st, and return to their sinful habit of not going to Mass on Sunday. You did nothing to help break their vice of living in a perpetual state of breaking the Commandments. And that's all the pathetic Church of Nice can muster in response.

Christmas is about nothing else than a little Baby. The fact that that Infant is God and He is here to save us from Hell doesn't even hit the radar of the Church of Nice leaders—and that's because talking about Hell and salvation isn't "nice."

Confused Catholic
Originally aired February 12, 2015

THE HITS JUST KEEP COMING. Now, we have one of the senior cardinals in the Church denying the miracles of Our Lord. Cardinal Walter Kasper in his retirement is becoming an ecclesiastical rock, and all for selling out Jesus Christ. He's not the first, certainly, and won't be the last—but he is the current sell-out, and he's not alone. These kinds never are.

Cardinal Kasper, who started the ball of chaos rolling at the 2014 Synod on the Family by saying adulterers should be admitted to Holy Communion, is claiming that Jesus' miracles didn't really happen. His words about the miracle accounts in the gospels: "We are faced not with historical details but with stylistic devices intended to attract the attention and raise excitement in the minds of those listening . . . ." And again, "The probability is that we need not take the so-called 'nature miracles' as historical."

This is all from his 1976 book *Jesus the Christ*, which is gaining new traction. And it is disgusting; it is filthy. He maintains that after the Resurrection and when the gospels were being written in the first century, the stories were changed to include miracles to bolster the claim that Jesus was divine. In short, the miracle stories, at least many of them, were made up, a kind of PR campaign for the little sect of Jews in the backwaters of the empire to gain some attention. And yes, this is all coming from the mouth of a prince of the Church. Not exactly princely, for a prince to deny truths about his King. But this is part and parcel of the current crisis and disaster that is denied or ignored or unknown by most Catholics today.

On one level, from purely a human standpoint, it all seems kind of reasonable: A bunch of followers are trying to brag it up about their dead leader, so they gild the lily a bit and push a few exaggerations, all for a good cause, of course. And that approach would reduce the Catholic faith to a mere human institution, with some minimal claim on some kind of spiritual something or other.

Kasper is not alone in this among prelates, priests, and laity. A surprisingly large number of them are surfacing, each nibbling away and bashing at one teaching after another: Holy Communion for adulterers, fake miracle accounts, same-sex "marriage" approval, "mercy" for contracepting couples, and on and on. It's enough to make a solid Catholic's head start to spin.

When we started our sister organization St. Michael's Media back in late 2005, we had in mind defending the Church from outside attacks. We were ignorant of the actual reality that the Church's real need for defense would be from traitors *inside* the Church. When that became evident, we kept up with producing St. Michael's Media's theological programming and started up what is now Church Militant to point out the treachery and heresy *within* the Church.

But that was never part of the original plan for this apostolate. It was always simply to promote the glory of the magisterial teaching of the Faith protected by the Holy Spirit. Sadly, that is difficult to do with so many traitorous, lazy, and cowardly clerics running things the way they do. They strangle and choke off various avenues within the Establishment Church to pass on the authentic faith. So what has arisen is a movement of faithful Catholics to call these specific clerics on their evil and do an end run around them by presenting the authentic faith free from their poison of false ecumenism, watered-down doctrine, worldly compromise, and outright denial of aspects of the Faith.

Faithful Catholics have tackled this issue in differing ways. We here at Church Militant are tackling this by producing programming true to the Faith. That is what our Premium channel is all about. If you are a Catholic and not deeply disturbed by stories like that of Cdl. Kasper's denial of the gospel miracles, then you aren't a serious Catholic, and Church Militant probably isn't for you. But if you are bothered by this, if you want to be part of the solution, if you want to deepen your faith and adopt the spirit of a Catholic warrior well prepared intellectually as well as spiritually, then you may find yourself more aligned with our work. Whatever the case, do your part to shore up the Faith against the attacks from within.

Flamethrower Catholicism
Originally aired June 1, 2015

T HE CHURCH IS RIDDLED WITH HERETICS and schismatics and dissidents, and it's time to bring out the blowtorch.

These individuals have nearly destroyed the Church; they are responsible for the loss of hundreds of millions of souls. Many of them are clergy, and an alarming number of them are bishops—men who are cowards, who the Holy Spirit says will be the type of person who will be the first to descend into Hell: cowards. Others are traitors—men who have no supernatural faith and work to overturn the truth of divine revelation.

It's like the Garden of Gethsemane all over again—cowardly bishops deserting or wicked bishops betraying Our Lord for personal profit. We see their handiwork at the 2014 synod in Rome and their conniving and scheming behind the scenes in preparation for the 2015 synod.

But this combination of cowards and traitors doesn't do its work only in the Church, although that is, of course, where the effect of their evil handiwork is most largely felt. The effect is also felt in society, in the culture at large, as evidenced in the referendum results from Ireland, where sodomite marriage was embraced by an appalling number of Catholics and a majority of the population in general. Eighty-five percent of Irish citizens are baptized Catholics. Sixty-two percent of Irish citizens voted against the Faith and in favor of sodomy as marriage.

How did this happen? In short, because of traitorous and cowardly bishops and the priests they ordained and put in parishes and schools. These bishops shied away from the hard confrontations they should have engaged in out of love for the truth, out of love for the Faith. They were too busy fomenting rebellion or looking the other way as those under them fomented it.

How much longer will the Church have to endure these homosexual bishops and cardinals who promote and advance homosexual priests, or those sympathetic to the militant homosexual agenda, all in the name of "mercy"? These homosexualists corrupt the Faith. They destroy and pervert and poison the Church.

And here is the answer to why there is so much evil in the world: because of these rotten, evil Churchmen. We pray, we hope they repent and return to the Faith, but in the meantime they need to be exposed for the evil they spread. We must always consider, however, that the Church is the soul of humanity, the life force of the world exactly because She was commissioned to be so by the Son of God. Her duty is to fight evil, advance the Truth—not to compromise with it, and certainly not to pave the way for its conquest of men's hearts.

But that's what these men have done. From the hierarchy of Ireland over the past fifty years right up to priests in the aftermath of the vote declaring that Catholics who opposed same-sex "marriage" need to go to confession, all this has happened because of unfaithful clergy. These men belong to Satan for the exact same reason that Our Blessed Lord said the Pharisees had Satan as their father: because they do his will.

Satan's primary activity is the destruction of the Catholic Church, the elimination of Catholics from the face of the earth. Less than 30 percent of Catholics in the land of St. Patrick now attend weekly Mass, and most of them are old. The hatred for the Faith among the young of Ireland is palpable, a deep-seated animosity. Although most of them are baptized, they have no knowledge or regard for the Church's beauty. This is directly attributable to the majority of bishops and their effeminate clergy who in many ways hate the Faith even more than many of the young.

And let's be very clear here: The young hate what they *believe* the Church to be. That doesn't let them off the hook, but they do labor under some degree of ignorance, however willful that ignorance might be. But the clergy, most especially the majority of bishops, *know* the Truth, and simply reject it.

They have hardened their hearts to the love of Our Lord and led their sheep to the brink of Hell, they being the first to plunge into the abyss. As Our Lord sternly warned, "If then the light in you is darkness, how great is the darkness!" (Matthew 6:23). These men sat by in silence or consent in the face of divorce. These men sat by in silence or consent in the face of contraception. These men sat by in silence or consent in the face of abortion. And now they have sat by in silence or consent in the face of sodomy. They have disfigured the face of Our Lord.

It's time for a divine flamethrower to be released where the mettle of these leaders can be fully revealed, where the faithful who don't have the stomach to face the reality of the evil in these men can see these men for who they truly are. They need to be unmasked; they need to be revealed. The Catholic world needs to know the whole truth. The Catholic faithful need to understand the corruption that lies within the souls of these men, these wolves in shepherds' clothing.

The Catholic Church is the only organization with divine authority to repel Satan and his works. When the men charged with leading the fight against Hell are actually double agents for Satan as revealed by their actions, it's time for Heaven to unleash the flamethrower of truth.

Whom Do You Love?
Originally aired July 16, 2015

HERE'S A TRICK QUESTION: Whom do you love more than anyone else in the whole wide world? Spouse? Children? Money, even?

If your answer is anything besides Our Lord, now you can begin to understand why the other side is so successful at always winning every major clash of the culture. There can only be three objects of love, and in fact, two of those objects are related. You can only love God and your neighbor *or* love yourself. There are no other options.

The other side is expert at loving self. It's exhibited in how deeply and seriously they pursue money, sex, power, fame, whatever. They wake up in the morning thinking about these things, thinking about self. They spend enormous amounts of energy throughout the day chasing these things, and they go to bed thinking about how they will chase these down tomorrow.

Talk about committed! Talk about a deep, undistracted desire! That is one committed bunch. It's why they are so successful at keeping abortion legal, getting same-sex "marriage" installed as a constitutional right, constantly engineering new and improved birth control while making it more accepted. They are experts in the art of self-love. And they are prepared to defend and promote their cause much better than we are. In fact, if this were a Super Bowl, we would get destroyed collectively.

Oh, wait—we *are* getting destroyed collectively.

The reason? They are prepared for battle, and we are not. Have you ever noticed, e.g., how the cause of evil can always mask itself so cleverly in a pithy slogan on a bumper sticker? *No Hate. Love Wins. Coexist. Save the Whales.* And then they've gotten so effective they don't even need words anymore. That equal sign, that Darwin fish, that rainbow—it won't be long before those stick people window decals showing a family and kids start appearing showing two "mommies" or two "daddies" with their IVF surrogate womb children in tow.

The world sits around thinking about this stuff non-stop. They discuss it at their parties, report on it in their media, unify themselves in their cause, take control of their political party (actually, both parties), elect their candidates, pump out their movies and TV shows. Why? Because they are committed and dedicated on a scale that we could only ever hope to imagine. They are better prepared than we are, and we lose every time because they are better prepared to defeat us than we are prepared to defeat them.

And just like in the Super Bowl, whoever is better prepared *wins*. It's almost guaranteed. Only dumb luck can prevent any other outcome—the ball bounces weird, their star gets injured, they get a lot of penalties, etc. The only way to defeat evil is to be better prepared than they are when it comes to the fight—just like it is in sports and war. And the only way to be better prepared is to be more dedicated and committed; and the only way to do that is to love Our Lord and His Holy Catholic Church more than they love them-selves.

We don't love the Church, truly love it and cling to it and embrace it and defend it—or, at least, not enough. As the song goes, "I would do anything for love." The other side does. We don't. It's that simple. How many hours do we spend in a week sitting down studying the Faith, seriously studying, committing ourselves to reading, meditating on what we have read, acquainting ourselves with the arguments of the other side so we can be prepared to respond when necessary and destroy their position intellectually?

How often can we be accused of loving so intently that people recognize us as mastering our own wills? Do people look at us and say, "Boy, he's changed. He seems more, I don't know, serious, mature"? What they mean is holy. They don't have the vocabulary to express that, but they recognize it.

We see a seemingly endless parade of people on the other side we would describe in a general sense or application of the term as "intense." They are studied; however mistaken they are in their intellects, they are well-studied. They have committed themselves entirely in their wills. They are devoted.

We aren't. We don't go the extra mile and read more. We don't go the extra mile and pray more. We don't seek out like-minded people and discuss more. We play too much in the world's sandbox—and then are saddened, horrified, shocked, when the Supreme Court hands down a perverted, evil, immoral ruling.

Until we get better prepared, which is to say love God by loving His Holy Bride with all our minds, hearts, souls, and strength, get used to more of the same. But when we *do* become committed, devoted, loving souls, watch out, world. Just watch out.

Crystal Ball Catholicism
Originally aired August 3, 2015

JUST IMAGINE WHAT SOCIETY TODAY would have looked like, could have looked like, if Church leaders had done their job for the past fifty years, had a vigorous defense been put up against the evil of contraception back in the 1960s—and even before the 1960s, if the American hierarchy had fought tooth and nail against no-fault divorce back in the day, and against Catholic politicians who supported it, would have flat out excommunicated most of the Kennedy clan when there was still something fearful and consequential about being excommunicated.

Imagine if the seminaries had been properly patrolled and monitored in the 1940s and 1950s to screen out men there for a hundred other reasons than love of souls. What if the catechetical garbage flowing out of Catholic publishers had been slam-dunked before it ever got in front of the eyes of a Catholic student? Or if women religious orders had been purged of feminazi lesbians just waiting their turn to get revenge on their male masters? Or if male religious orders had been purged from the seminaries of effeminate men looking for a psychosexual drama outlet and a place to meet like-minded men?

Imagine for just a moment what the culture would look like if we had real men battling the plague of homosexuality in the culture back in the 1970s instead of prelates like Cdl. Joseph Bernadin in Chicago and Cdl. John Dearden in Detroit embracing that subculture; if we had prelates who could recognize the spiritual meltdown occurring instead of helping it along; if they'd been surrounded by men and women who actually cared for the Faith more than for them-selves and their interests and pet projects.

How would bishops have been served so much better by those

around them if their staff hadn't been so concerned about becoming bishops themselves? What would things be like now if there had been real men who loved and believed in Our Lord's Real Presence in the Blessed Sacrament, instead of those who had lost their supernatural faith? Where would the culture be now if valiant men, virtuous men, had shouted from the rooftops and pounded on pulpits that truth is truth and evil is evil no matter how either may appear?

What if politicians had to pay a price among Catholic voters for their choice to support evil? What would the world look like today if presidents and clergy at Catholic universities had kept true to their identities instead of polluting young Catholics' minds? How incredible, how far removed from the darkness would our families and loved ones be now if only . . . if only . . . ? And how much greater would the likelihood be now that many of these men back in the day might not have been damned, if they were?

Moving forward, Catholics today have been given a world drowning in evil because of Catholics of yesteryear and the men they trained to run the show. The question is, therefore, look into your crystal ball down the road and ask yourself: What will Catholics of the next generations say about me and how I acted today in the name of the Church?

And don't forget: By the time the future rolls around and they ask that question of us, Our Blessed Lord will have already answered it for us. And the answer will be either Heaven or Hell.

Vocabulary Diarrhea: Bishop Babble
Originally aired October 8, 2015

THERE ISN'T REALLY ANY OTHER WAY to say this: A group of poorly trained ideological bishops have come to Rome to try and change whatever they want to or can with regard to Church teaching. It's being disguised as kind of tweaking around the edges, but if these men have their way, the Church may look more Protestant than Catholic.

And the funny thing: All the proponents of change keep repeating that there is no division; everything is peaceful inside the Hall; everyone is getting along just fine. Sadly, that may very well in fact be the case because from what has been officially relayed so far, it's been one nutty idea after another. It seems as if anything goes at this Synod on the Family:

- Holy Communion for the divorced and remarried
- General absolution for everyone
- A new catechetical approach for those living in sin
- An end to mean, exclusionary language calling sin sin and sinners sinners
- Letting different parts of the world determine different approaches to dogma
- The ordination of women to the diaconate
- Avoiding calling sinful situations what they are because those are negative judgments

This is crazy, and it's only the first week still. Talk about the beginning of woes. A step or two more to the left and they'll be nominating Hillary for pope. And then one of the primary agents of change, Germany's Cdl. Reinhard Marx, comes out and has the audacity to blame the *media* for creating this storm of controversy. Talk about gall.

For the record, or rather to correct the record, the media, including us, are talking to bishops, reading their interviews, listening to what's being reported at the daily press briefings. We aren't making this stuff up. For example, Abp. Paul-André Durocher gave an interview where he said women should be ordained to the diaconate.

Here's what's so crazy about this whole affair: that so many bishops from all over the place would feel so free to sound off like this. And for those anxious to blast the pope and blame him for all, remember, almost all these men were bishops *before* Pope Francis came along, and it's a pretty safe bet they did not just start holding these nutty opinions. They may feel freer to express them now given the self-admitted lack of precise language evident in this papacy, but they thought all these thoughts long before anyone ever heard of Pope Francis.

How bad are things? These men took an oath of fidelity to the Church, to Her teachings, and to defend and promote them. Yet somehow they were promoted to the office of bishop—*all over the world*. Not all of them are bad, proposing heresy and nutjob ideas to solve the crisis—the crisis they all helped create—but enough of them are so far off the reservation that, at this point, we're waiting for one of them to stand up in the Hall and propose that God retire and they'll take over.

Canadian archbishop Durocher has repeatedly condemned, for example, the idea of a "Catholic ghetto," meaning walling ourselves in, not being accessible to the world. He forgets it is not the job of the Church to make itself accessible to the fallen world; it is the job of the Church to rush headlong into the world and change it, convert it, save it, and smash Satan in the mouth on the way out the door.

Why is this so hard for these men to figure out? A Catholic ghetto? Really? What a weird analogy. Why not use the analogy of a Catholic castle shining on a hill? Why not use the analogy that St. Teresa of Avila used of a great castle of crystal with various rooms? See, using the word "ghetto" makes it seem all icky and ugly and doom-and-gloom and desperate.

There is nothing "ghetto" about the Bride of Christ. That is a poor sociological term misapplied to Holy Mother Church.

And as an aside, the way the archbishop used the term doesn't even make sense in the natural world. Those faith groups that have "ghettoized" themselves—which really means to insulate themselves against the evils of the world—haven't done so poorly in their approach. In his native Canada, the Amish "ghetto dwellers" are doubling their size every generation, while his Canadian Church is shrinking into oblivion. So when we are talking all over the place about dialogue and accompanying every single person on earth with every single issue they have every single step of the way, perhaps someone in the Synod should be assigned to the Canadian Amish to figure out how they have done so well at passing on the Faith in their ghetto. Isn't that supposed to be the point of this Synod anyway—to figure out how to help families pass on the Faith amidst all the challenges of the contemporary world?

What's happening here is a diarrhea of vocabulary, a case of the verbal runs, where the point seems to be to ooze out as many weird verbal concoctions as possible and ramble on for as long as possible using all kinds of sophisticated, high-sounding platitudes of nonsense, which at the end of the day don't say a darn thing, or mean anything, but have the predictable effect of being able to be spun any way you want so the faithful can be as confused as you can possibly make them.

Take, for example, the intervention offered on Tuesday by Antwerp bishop Johan Bonny, the bishop who wants the Church to bless sodomite marriages. You can't make this stuff up, folks.

The experiences of our contemporaries are diverse and varied. More than in the past, their life stories follow a personal course. Next to risks and limitations, this development also offers possibilities and opportunities. It is important that the Church highlight the positive or constructive elements in this development, value the "seeds of the Words" which are dormant in life stories, recognize the graduality in the process of growth that people go through, respect and promote the "divine pedagogy of grace" on the path of life that God goes with people, and also welcome a *praeparatio evangelica* in the "symphony of differences," and especially to end all exclusions.

See what we mean? I'm not sure Bp. Bonny even knows what he means.

This collegiality-driven bishop babble has got to be called out because it is damaging the faithful. It's destructive to souls; it's probably even heretical if you could begin to figure out what's being said.

Chapter Four

Contraception & Abortion

N O SINGLE ISSUE IN THE CHURCH in America has revealed the fault line between faithful and unfaithful Catholics (clergy and laity alike) than the issue of contraception; abortion is just the natural consequence of contraception. Since the 1960s, Catholic clerics in the United States, most especially the hierarchy, have remained almost silent on the intrinsic evil of contraception.

This has resulted in devastation not only to life on a temporal plane, which Bd. Pope Paul VI predicted in his landmark encyclical *Humanae Vitae* in July 1968, but it has wiped out the life of the Church in the United States: considerably smaller families, dramatically fewer Catholic marriages, a steep plunge in priestly and religious vocations resulting in a meltdown of teaching orders that, in turn, resulted in the closing of thousands of Catholic parish schools and high schools, and skyrocketing costs for those that are left, effectively pricing out all but the more well-to-do. And now, almost four generations of a shrinking and declining Catholic population is being felt like an earthquake, as diocese after diocese scrambles for funds while closing parishes in cycle after cycle every ten years or so.

All of this is owing to the bishops' silence on contraception, something they should be terrified of when thinking about their own judgments before the Supreme Shepherd. But even more devastating has been the resulting loss of Catholic identity. At what might be considered the height of the Sexual Revolution from 1965–1975, at the very moment Catholics needed their shepherds to proclaim the truth, the bishops backed away. Today's bishops have done nothing to correct the evil they've inherited; in fact, they've institutionalized it.

The Bishops and Sex
Originally aired July 12, 2011

IN A NUTSHELL, HERE IS THE PROBLEM in the Church in the West: Contraception is not condemned by the vast majority of bishops the way it should be.

Practically every evil besetting the Church these days is owing to this single cancer. The deafening silence on the part of the shepherds has been interpreted as a wink and a nod that unfruitful sex is ok. That has caused a chain reaction, a violent reaction, throughout the land of the faithful. Everything has flowed from this one act of neglect: divorce, abortion, embryonic stem cell research, homosexuality, and the attendant evils of each.

Contraception, it now seems, was destined to become the nail in the coffin for the Church in the West. The refusal to teach about it in any substantive manner by the bishops, the on-the-ground dismissal of the teaching by hordes of priests in parishes, the resulting widespread acceptance of it by the laity—all of this has brought down the entire house. With rare exception here and there, almost nothing is left. No one, including Church leaders, can even fake surprise that homosexuality is so openly accepted by the average Catholic. This fact alone proves the absolutely dismal, horrendous job of teaching the Faith that has gone on in the past, and to be blunt, is still the case.

Of course homosexuality is going to be accepted, and so-called homosexual "marriage," because for a laity largely raised on the superstitions of secular humanism, how can they see any fault with it, other than perhaps a personal gross-out factor? Once contraceptive sex is allowed, then why can't homosexual sex be allowed as well? Contraception divorces the act from its purpose, which is having children. When the mentality reigns supreme that sex doesn't have to do with procreation, then it's "Nellie, bar the doors."

The reasonable but unconvincing arguments that homosexual couples—men or women—don't or can't love each other or aren't interested in children just don't cut it. Don't waste your breath making an appeal to matters of taxation or increased pension costs or health costs or any other financial or economic arguments. In the end, two men or two women can be just as "in love"—meaning a feeling—as one man and one woman.

Marriage was once upon a time considered a vocation, a commitment of one's life. Now, it's just a lifestyle two people share based on their sexual complementarity. This is because of contraception. The contraceptive mentality has destroyed more than just the understanding of marriage. It has corrupted the very practice of marriage, how it is lived in the real world. So now today, the culture—the same culture in which Catholics live and breathe—has been prepared to see marriage as just an arrangement built around sex and emotion, where assets are lumped together and the whole thing might or might not have something to do with children. With that new definition, why can't two gays or lesbians get married?

If it isn't called a sin, if the underlying contraceptive mentality that supports this perverted sense of marriage isn't attacked at its root, then there really is nothing for the bishops to say. It's no use saying that marriage is a good thing and let's keep it that way when so many people no longer see marriage the way the Catholic Church does. And the reason they don't is because too many bishops and too many priests simply will not call a spade a spade and a sin a sin.

When they give up that vocabulary, which is the truth, and start trafficking in the language and vocabulary of the world, they may as well stay silent, finish gathering up the collections from the few remaining elderly people sitting in the pews, and turn out the lights when the last one dies. The reason Our Blessed Lord gave the shepherds such incredible authority is for them to use it. Failing this, we get all the evils that come upon us.

The Deadly Compromise
Originally aired May 15, 2015

THE CULTURE TOLERATES the pro-life movement because the pro-life movement has acquiesced on the subject of contra-ception. So, for example, in U.S. politics, the Republican Party leadership allows the anti-abortion rhetoric to come forward every election season knowing that nothing much will come of it. They allow it in exchange for votes and financial contributions, but in the end, nothing changes—and that's fine with them.

And in the larger context, it's all right to have prayer rallies and demonstrations and even a big annual march (which gets zero coverage in the secular world) because the pro-life movement will never challenge contraception, which is the root of all this. It won't challenge it because it would reveal the deep religious differences between many Catholics and many contraception-embracing protestants in the movement.

The quiet compromise in the movement that has taken place is: The lives of babies are more important than the larger truth. That is now the ironclad position of the pro-life movement, molded and shaped by a tenuous and false political ecumenism. And when that compromised position is brought to the table of the struggle with the united secular forces, a further compromise is exacted. March and demonstrate all you want. We will just ignore you.

This same principle of compromise exists now with many leaders in the Catholic Church, who have simply thrown in the towel on the issue of sexual morality and have compromised with the forces of darkness. And at the core of their cowardly compromise is, again, the issue of contraception. They have rebelled in their silence since the days of Bd. Pope Paul VI's *Humanae Vitae*.

For going on fifty years, weak, feminized leaders have refused to go to the mat over this issue—as even Cdl. Timothy Dolan of New York confessed to the *Wall Street Journal* in an interview. They either don't want to see or don't have the requisite native intelligence to see the connection between contraception and the entire typhoon of evil engulfing Western civilization. No attempts at evangelization will work, because people want their birth control pill and their porn. So the bishops have merely accepted this and have spent a half-century now trying to preach joy and other nonsense approaches without going to the gallows denouncing sin. Imagine if John the Baptist had used their approach. "Um, excuse me, Herod; I have something to tell you that you don't want to hear, so I won't say it. Instead, look how joyful I am. Want some locust? How about a little honey to follow it up?"

What has happened to the world is what happens when the Church is punished with weak leaders. Even now, amidst all the craziness, we have still further craziness: Bishop Johan Bonny in Belgium saying we should have the "sacrament" of gay weddings; another European bishop defending funerals for dogs; a near-majority of the German bishops saying give Holy Communion to non-Catholics.

All of these evils have come about because of contraception. Sex has been placed in the category of existing for personal pleasure and little else. The capitulation of so many Catholic leaders on this single point has been the undoing of the Faith in the hearts of hundreds of millions of Catholics, and will be the reason the Church will be undergoing Her forthcoming persecution.

It is only a temporary illusion that Church leaders can compromise with the world. Evil never wants a compromise. It always wants more and more and more until it controls everything. That is the same attitude the Church should have. The reality that we are in a struggle to the death with the powers of Hell just doesn't seem to resonate with so many of these cowardly leaders anymore, if it ever did.

The only way now to get Satan out of the crannies and crevices he occupies in the Church will be to see him step out in full force, to witness the mask coming off and witness the unleashing of his hatred against the faithful. This has all moved beyond any human, natural means to save it. It's time for divine intervention to bring an end to the deadly compromise.

Dark Knights
Originally aired June 11, 2015

THE MAIN PROBLEM that Knights of Columbus complain about is a lack of fidelity to the Faith among members at various levels of leadership, most especially at the national level, although it's not exclusive to that. These concerns have developed something of a track record in the past twenty years or so as the culture of death and evil has accelerated.

Many knights think the organization needs to respond more vigorously and aggressively to that culture first and foremost within its own ranks, where horrible catechesis along with indifference toward and even acceptance of the general cultural evils is too common, with too much emphasis on continuing to bring in billions of dollars in insurance money each year.

The top brass at the Knights of Columbus receive huge paychecks, with Supreme Knight Carl Anderson getting paid more than $2 million a year. While there is nothing intrinsically wrong with being wealthy, it does raise eyebrows among more faithful Catholics who wonder: Is the Faith being compromised in order not to rock the boat of the lucrative insurance business?

In earlier times, members of the Knights of Columbus were concerned that pro-abortion politicians were being allowed to stay in the organization. National headquarters shut down that discussion, refusing to let local councils remove members from their ranks. The reason national leadership gave was that the bishops hadn't excommunicated these politicians, therefore they wouldn't, either.

Bad reasoning. First, the Knights of Columbus is a lay-run organization with its own set of bylaws. It is free to do what it wants with members. Second, being chucked out of the Knights has nothing to do with excommunication. You can be expelled for failing to pay your annual dues—and last we checked, not keeping up with your dues does not warrant excommunication. Third, to appeal to the bishops' failure to take action is a red herring. Members who are admitted to the Knights didn't need the bishops' approval. Why should it then be the case that it's the bishops who must declare them out? It's a smokescreen.

In June 2011, the gay marriage debate was raging in New York. The vote in the New York Senate was down to the slimmest of margins. Fake Catholic Andrew Cuomo, who hates the Church's teachings, was governor. He needed the two remaining holdouts in the state senate to vote in favor of gay marriage, or else it would be defeated—that's how close the vote was.

The two remaining holdouts were state senators Joe Addabbo and David Carlucci. Each man is a member of the Knights of Columbus, and they each ended up casting their vote in favor of sodomite marriage.

Senator David Carlucci eventually went on to garner some more fame and cheers from the homofascist crowd by ripping into a 75-year-old town clerk, Barbara MacEwan from Volney, New York, who said she didn't want to sign the marriage certificates herself once sodomite marriage became legal. Carlucci used the occasion to grandstand in the media, positioning himself as the great defender of the law—a law he may very well have sold his soul to get enacted.

MacEwan didn't say her office wouldn't sign them, just that *she* didn't want to sign them personally because she disagreed with it in conscience. Nevertheless, she understood that her office had to sign them, and she agreed that her office would; but she herself would not. A deputy clerk would be assigned the task. That didn't stop Knight of Columbus Carlucci from publicly raking this 75-year-old female civil servant over the coals for his own gain. Yet at no point did the Knights of Columbus say a public word in her defense.

Then there is Sen. Joe Addabbo, the other turncoat knight whose vote was needed to make sodomite marriage secure. Interesting and noteworthy in his case especially is that before he voted yes for gay marriage, he had voted no two years earlier. So here is a man who did the right thing, then turned around and did the demonstrably wrong thing. And, of course, not a word from national leadership.

As the homofascist agenda continues to gain momentum to the point of now forcing ordinary people to submit to its perversions, the Knights are going to encounter this dilemma more and more. So far, they are failing spectacularly, as Knights of Columbus halls are being rented out for lesbian weddings and local councils are permitting it, hiding behind the fear of lawsuits.

Hey, Knights, be men for a change, like you once were, and just say no. If you get sued, who cares? Better to enter Heaven with a lawsuit in your hand than Hell with loads of cash.

Appeasement. Compromise. Collapse.
Originally aired August 28, 2015

N O DOUBT ABOUT IT, the Church in America is beyond retreat. And what has brought it to its knees is the curse of Americanism first widely proposed by Jesuit priest John Courtney Murray.

Going back many decades, the leadership of the Church in America, the hierarchy, was as concerned about having a place at the table of the American ruling class as it was about converting Americans to the Faith. Two forces clashed: (1) the fierce independence of Americanism and its philosophical baggage of a pluralistic society, where all religions and philosophies should have an equal voice, and (2) the Catholic Church, which—established by Almighty God as the only and one true religion—can never accept the situation in principle that all religions are worthy.

So these two orthodoxies smashed into each other in the so-called Great American Experiment—and the Church lost, because Her leaders were too concerned about being welcomed than converting the country. That trend has continued unabated for nearly 200 years. There never was any great wave of conversions, according to the bishops' own official tallies stretching back over a hundred years.

As many Catholics will attest, huge numbers of priests are simply unconcerned about trying to convert people to the Faith, which is why all this hullabaloo about the New Evangelization will produce sparse fruit. There is too much accommodation and not enough singling out of the greatness and uniqueness of Catholicism—in short, little direct, hard truth, an attitude that permeates the entire structure of the Church in America that we must get along, never give offense, and welcome any faith into the Big Tent of American Catholicism.

Case in point: The annual March for Life is clearly taking steps toward this goal, thinking that expanding the number of marchers is somehow a good thing in and of itself, regardless of the weakening of Catholic identity. That would come as a gross miscarriage in the eyes of Nellie Gray, who started the March back in 1974.

Gray was an avid Catholic and reached out to fellow Catholics, realizing instinctively that it would have to be rank-and-file Catholics to take the lead because Protestants had been compromised in their ability to defend life owing to their acceptance of contraception, which is the forerunner of abortion. Today's leaders are willing to paper over that enormous difference and go with the flow.

We see the same thing occurring at the 2015 World Meeting of Families in Philadelphia. Many faithful Catholics were stunned to find out that Philly archbishop Charles Chaput sanctioned pro-aborts and pro-sodomite marriage high-rollers as being on the leadership team of the prestigious conference.

It's billed as an ecumenical event, or at least is presented that way, owing to the various speakers who are not Catholic. It's a Catholic event run by a Catholic archdiocese. Why are Planned Parenthood financial supporters, sodomite-marriage cheerleaders, and big-money Party of Death politicians anywhere near this event? Why is it necessary to have Protestant speakers? Are there not enough faithful Catholics with various degrees and expertise to talk intelligently on these topics? Are there not enough influential Catholic money-men who would be honored to be chosen to be on the leadership team?

All this constant stream of accommodation, appeasement, cooperation with the culture stems from this twisted notion of Americanism, wanting to be liked by the culture so much that you continually give up part of your identity, until in the end there's nothing—no *thing*—of you left.

Yet today's American hierarchy is all in with this Americanist heresy. They have been schooled and malformed from their seminary days back in the 1970s and 1980s that you have to go along to get along and never rock the boat. In a multi-cultural society, that means never standing up and declaring the authority and rightness of the Catholic Church. That's why so many Church of Nice Catholics and leaders have gone off the rails with their support of social justice efforts. They have joined with the worldly-minded who see worldly causes as the most important, supplanting the spiritual.

The perfect example is Cdl. Blase Cupich (then archbishop) of Chicago, who issued a statement in response to the grisly Planned Parenthood aborted baby parts videos, where he said that "we should be no less appalled" by joblessness.

This is spiritual insanity, the whole lot of it—constant compromise, continual appeasement, wanting desperately to be invited to the party and hang with the cool kids. For the love of God, realize your dignity as successors of the Apostles and have the guts to stand up like men and assert the glory of the Faith! Tell people this is the One True Faith. Tell them those other man-made religions offer no salvation. Tell them the moralities they profess are founded on shifting sands and will lead to their ruination as a people.

Who cares if you have a big, splashy affair that lasts a couple of days in Philadelphia? What will it have accomplished after the crowd has gone home? Will any souls have come to the truth of Our Blessed Lord's Church? Will any souls already in the Church have realized the extent of cultural and diabolical evil they have bought into and commit to changing their lives—to giving up contraception, to stop receiving Holy Communion in a state of mortal sin, to stop supporting loved ones in their sins of homosexuality and cohabitation?

That's all that matters, nothing else: that people come to accept the Catholic Church as the only means of salvation and they come into or be renewed in it, that they discover or renew a deep love for Our Blessed Lord, that they desire to encounter Him in the sacraments.

How many souls will walk in and out of the convention center, surrounded by Catholics, and never once be challenged to surrender their nutty American notion that all religions are worthy and we should all just get along? It's time for bishops to surrender their allegiance to John Courtney Murray's vision of the Church and begin to establish a kingdom that Jesus Christ came to establish. And you can bet *that* kingdom does not include supporters of child murder and sodomy on its leadership team.

It's All About Contraception
Originally aired January 20, 2016

IT'S TIME ONCE AGAIN for the annual March for Life in Washington, D.C., where hundreds of thousands of well-intentioned folks come to protest the slaughter of little children, demanding the law be changed. But how did it come to pass that killing children in the womb is now protected by the law?

Like everything, you have to go back to the beginning to get the full picture. Owing to the massive movement of soldiers, the U.S. Civil War gave rise to the first large-scale beginnings of pornography as an industry. Pornographic materials and literature, such as they were in the post-Civil War era, had kickstarted a weakening of morals.

In 1873, the U.S. Congress passed a law called the "Suppression of Trade in, and Circulation of, Obscene Literature and Articles of Immoral Use." It was championed by Anthony Comstock and thereafter was called simply the Comstock Law.

It was a federal law, but more than half the states adopted it. Among other things, Comstock outlawed abortifacients and contraceptives. Comstock was essentially the law of the land for nearly a century; but it began drawing heated opposition in the early 1900s from the burgeoning birth control movement, largely spearheaded by women.

In 1961, Estelle Griswold opened a Planned Parenthood clinic in New Haven, Connecticut and was eventually convicted for dispensing birth control to married women. She lost every appeal of her conviction except the only one that mattered: the U.S. Supreme Court.

On June 7, 1965, four years after opening her clinic, in the 7–2 decision *Griswold v. Connecticut*, the justices ruled that married couples have a constitutional right to contraception. They cited the Fifth, Ninth, and Fourteenth Amendments as the basis for their ruling.

In the majority opinion, Justice William O. Douglas held that a right to contraception among married couples exists owing to "penumbras" and "emanations" in the fabric of the Constitution. Those are legal terms meaning, in short, things you can assume and interpret in a manner that will allow more than the actual law says. The *Griswold* case also established a right to privacy—and now you can see where this is all going to arrive.

In 1972, in another Supreme Court case, *Eisenstadt v. Baird*, the case was argued and eventually won that it is a violation of the Equal Protection Clause of the Fourteenth Amendment to allow married couples to use contraception and deny that "right" to *unmarried* couples. The vote of the justices was again 7–2.

Exactly ten months to the day after the *Eisenstadt* ruling, the same justices voted (again 7–2) that the same arguments to allow contraception also allow a woman to kill the baby in her womb. That was *Roe v. Wade*.

Everything about abortion is about contraception. Almost half of women who get abortions do so because their contraception failed, a little-realized point that keeps Planned Parenthood and its allies constantly pushing birth control. Failed contraception leads to unintended pregnancy, which leads to abortion in half the cases.

Contraception establishes a thought process in the minds of people that sex doesn't necessarily relate to conception, which is where the word "contraception" comes from: *contra* (against) conception. A person, especially a Catholic, cannot decry abortion while permitting, supporting, or ignoring contraception.

Yet many people do, even those at the heart of the self-styled pro-life movement. If you are against abortion but permit contraception, then you are not pro-life. All you are is pro-birth. That is *not* Catholic, and no amount of pretense will make it so.

Visit From a Demon
Originally aired April 11, 2016

IT SHOULD COME AS NO SURPRISE that abortion and contraception are from Hell. But something almost no one knows is the demonic presence testified to by one of the world's leading contraception proponents back in the earliest days of the movement.

Marie Stopes was to England what Margaret Sanger was to the United States: a woman crazed over the idea of making birth control accepted and welcomed owing to her racist passions. Sanger is responsible for Planned Parenthood, which kills 3.8 million children through abortion worldwide every year. Stopes is largely responsible for Marie Stopes International, which kills 3.1 million children through abortion worldwide every year.

The two met at a conference in England in 1915. Stopes was a respected academic, the first female professor at the University of Manchester. But around 1910, when she was 30 years old, she became enthralled with eugenics and wanted to reduce the number of "undesirables" in society. She began petitioning various leaders in England, most of whom gave her the cold shoulder, despite her academic credentials.

In 1917 she published a book, *Married Love*, promoting birth control, which was so popular it went through five printings in the first year. Still, the ruling class remained unimpressed, most especially the leaders of the Church of England, who in 1920 were gathering for their scheduled meeting in Lambeth Palace, which took place every ten years. Shortly before the meeting, Stopes herself relayed that a voice spoke to her while she was sitting in the shade of a yew tree in her backyard.

The voice, she claimed, was the voice of God, telling her to relay to the bishops that they were to change the teaching on birth control. She dashed into the house and dictated to her secretary: "My Lords, I speak to you in the name of God. You are his priests. I am his prophet."

And so began a work she eventually titled *A New Gospel to All Peoples: A Revelation of God Uniting Physiology and the Religions of Man*. It was completed by the summer and a copy sent to each of the 267 bishops at the Lambeth Conference.

In her work, she contradicted St. Paul, saying his message was 1,900 years old and could now be ignored, and added: "God spoke to *me* today."

She claimed God told her sexual union was not for procreation but for pleasure, that couples should use the best means of birth control "placed at man's service by Science." Stopes's vision or voice was certainly not from God, obviously, but she never denied or recanted the account. She heard a voice directing her what to do. She insisted that a supernatural voice, which she claimed was God, had given her instructions to spread birth control throughout the country and eventually the world.

She told the bishops in her letter that the voice had said the bishops must teach their flocks that "the pure and holy sacrament of marriage may no longer be debased and befouled by the archaic ignorance of the centuries . . . ." Sexual union was for pleasure, not procreation.

At Lambeth in 1920, despite the first shiftings of public opinion, the Church of England leaders rejected Stopes's vision and voices. Undeterred, Stopes published her New Gospel for the masses in 1922. It cost her dearly among her atheist university peers, who lost all respect for her and her claims to divine visions.

A year before publishing the *New Gospel*, she opened England's first birth control clinic, but shortly thereafter moved it to Whitfield Street near Tottenham Court Road. This site still remains an active birth control clinic as well as abortion counseling center. Like this central London clinic, Margaret Sanger had launched her country's first clinic in Brooklyn, New York five years earlier in 1916, making 2016 a kind of 100th anniversary of the public beginnings of the birth control movement.

Both women detested the Catholic Church and made no bones about saying so publicly. In 1942, Stopes remarked in writing that Catholics were "a curse, or something worse."

So when we sit back for a moment and consider that from these two women's actions, what they set in motion—around 7 million children killed worldwide every year—they both hated the Catholic Church, and one of them was inspired to greater zeal in her evil efforts by a supernatural voice she says directed her to spread the message that sex is about pleasure and not procreation.

Shortly before she heard the demonic voice, Stopes sent a copy of her book *Married Love* to Queen Mary, with an accompanying note saying that the book was written "in the interest, primarily, of your subjects, the British, but ultimately for the whole of Humanity."

Shortly afterward, she opened her birth control clinic, kept publishing articles in papers, writing more books, making inroads with political and religious leaders wherever she could. She carried on intensely for the next ten years, until the next Lambeth gathering of the Church of England leaders in 1930.

This time, however, the Church of England, for the first time in Christian history, approved of birth control—a decision arrived at, in large part, by the zeal of a woman spurred on by the voice of a demon.

Chapter Five

Government

A S IS BLINDINGLY CLEAR throughout all history, the power of the State has been brought to bear against the Catholic Church, sometimes obviously, other times less so. Occasionally, there have been brief respites from the war between Caesar and Christ, but they do not last for long. And when they resume, Caesar is usually bloodthirsty.

If one were to survey the twentieth century alone, the number of Catholic martyrs at the hands of the State, or more precisely, states, has been breathtaking. Millions of followers of Christ have been dispatched into eternity at the hands of dictators and brutal governments. One shudders to think of the number of those Catholics who gave up their earthly lives under Communist governments alone.

But in addition to red martyrdom at the hands of governments, there is also the more subtle "frog in the slowly boiling pot" approach by governments to assign the Church the place of little else than a historical footnote. As paganism reasserts itself in former Christian lands and nations, these white martyrdoms are sure to increase along a broad path, and there is a growing body of legal precedent.

What little of the Faith is left among Catholics after the destructive work of evil priests and bishops should be a small task for governments—extolling the anti-Catholic Enlightenment "virtues" of equality, fraternity, and liberty—to finish off. As Servant of God Fr. John Hardon said repeatedly, while Christ promised His Church would never be defeated, He did not guarantee it would not be defeated in a particular geography. There is much evidence throughout history to prove that claim, and the agent normally used by the Demon is the government.

The Pro-Life Problem
Originally aired November 26, 2012

I N HIS EVANGELIZING WORK, St. Paul said of Our Blessed Lord: "In him we live and move and have our being" (Acts 17:28). He was actually quoting a Greek poet from 500 years earlier but was able to expand on that thought and bring home its reality in relation to Christ.

Today, the pro-life movement is at a crossroads, especially the Catholic pro-life movement. So much attention, all of it well-intentioned, has been focused on changing laws that the real work of Catholics has been sidelined. We have a kind of bumper sticker mentality now: "God is pro-life." Spoken more accurately, He isn't so much pro-life as He *is* life—what St. Paul said.

From a spiritual point of view God *is* life. He is also Love, which means there is an equality and sameness to life and love—authentic Life and authentic Love, that is. Being pro-life from a political point of view is nearly meaningless. For goodness' sake, even an atheist can be pro-life—and many are. But while they are right politically, they miss the point entirely, and so, unfortunately, do some Catholics in the pro-life movement.

Politics should be the secondary goal. You can't change a culture by passing laws. Laws are a reflection of what the culture wants. Laws follow after the fact; they almost never lead the way. That's why same-sex "marriage" will be the law of the land. Enough people have been desensitized to the evil and immorality of homosexual sex, through the media largely, that its legal enshrinement is already a foregone conclusion.

Catholics, leaders and laity alike, need to concentrate more on what the Faith commands—that's what formed Christendom in the first place, and then the laws followed. Too many compromises happen in the political world because politicians' first and last concerns are usually their careers.

Abortion is still present in part because of all the compromises on such things as rape, incest, and the life of the mother.

But much of this is a result of the third-rail issue of contraception. Too many Catholics in the movement laid aside key and non-negotiable issues about their faith in order to accomplish a political end—a well-intended end—but one destined to fail. Crowing about incremental advances here and there in the states, or some particular funding program in some federal cases in this court or that, in the end amounts to nothing. At the end of the day, *Roe v. Wade* will remain protected and enshrined, and that, as they say, will be that.

Catholics need to go back to the drawing board and realize that our first duty is to save souls, not bodies—even the bodies of children. If souls are in a state of grace, then there would be no abortion. Remember, Satan doesn't care about killing children. If they wind up in Limbo for eternity, in a state of eternal bliss, although they're deprived of the Beatific Vision, they are still out of Satan's grasp. He's willing to give up those souls so that he can create murderers out of mothers and doctors and fathers—and from that he gains considerably. He creates a world that grows coarse to life and love and therefore God, Who is the source and end of each.

The souls of those little ones are kind of a loss leader for the diabolical, something in his calculus he might be willing to take a pass on if he can create a world indifferent to God, a world that's grown cold to life and love. And this shows forth a perfect example of how when the Church fails, evil advances. There is always a correlation between the world and the Church because Our Blessed Lord established an intimacy between the two.

The world is the theater of redemption. It is where the fruits of the redemption are applied. God so loved he world that He sent His only begotten Son. So it is the Church's solemn duty, grace, and privilege to convert the world. But it is a sure mark of failure when Church leaders begin efforts to educate politicians and not the flock. What else does God mean by the psalm "Put not your trust in princes" (Psalms 146:3)? And again, "The war horse is a vain hope for victory, and by its great might it cannot save" (Psalms 33:17).

Catholics in America have grown up in a spirit of compromise. This has translated into efforts even in the pro-life movement. Too many have looked at a political and cultural goal and compromised on the Faith. As long as contraception is acceptable to people who say they follow Christ, there will never be a rule of peace on earth. The mindset that allows the perversion of truth in this regard will inevitably spill over into a perversion of truth in other areas like life, religion, a correct understanding of liberty, objective morality.

The Church in the West has simply looked for the easy way to accomplish the political goal of ending abortion. Abortion isn't the problem; the acceptance of error is, as well as the lack of concern for total Catholic truth. There should have been mass conversion to the Catholic faith by well-meaning Protestants within the pro-life movement for all these years if Catholics were paying attention to the faith in its fullest sense. Yet many splendid leaders in the movement remain unconverted to the Faith. Have any Catholics ever sat down and talked with them about their souls?

No ecumenical effort with a religion that accepts theological compromise will ever be successful in the long run. It might score a political coup here or there, but the forces of darkness will just regroup and come back stronger, and the movement will be ill-prepared to cope with the stronger assault because it will not have dealt with its own internal struggle.

The Church did not convert the emperor; it converted the empire by converting the citizens.

Freedom of the Press
Originally aired February 20, 2015

WHEN AMERICA'S FOUNDING FATHERS sat down to formalize the principles of self-government, one of the first ones that got written down was freedom of the press. In fact, so much did they value transparency that it is the only profession explicitly stated in the Constitution—and not only stated, but actually guaranteed: feedom of the press—and in the long run of human history, it's still somewhat of a novel concept.

While it did enjoy some prominence in isolated pockets in the seventeenth century, it found its most enduring expression in the United States. So while it's not a uniquely American idea, it does have an American stamp on it. When it comes to mixing theology and the press, some interesting points arise. Specifically, when Catholicism runs headlong into a free press, fireworks can ignite.

The simple truth is this: Many leaders in the Church have no idea how to relate to the concept of freedom of the press. For many years, especially in the most recent decades, much of the damage done inside the Church has been able to happen because of secrecy and a Byzantine system of accountability. One need look no further than the homosexual clergy sex abuse scandal for evidence.

It was a "none of your business" attitude and "protect the system" approach and "don't cause scandal" mentality that allowed that evil not only to exist but to flourish for decades. Lawsuits with total awards in the billions and new legislation have largely tamped down the sex abuse itself, but the prevailing attitudes have gone nowhere. Everyday Catholics still encounter a system of privilege and access and clerical- ism like never before.

While the need for reform certainly existed in the whole sex abuse world, it was really the corporate approach that allowed this to fester that needed reform, and on that score, nothing has really happened. The notion of organized

Catholics with all the tools of the press approaching the Church from the perspective of demanding accountability is an entirely new phenomenon in the Church. Understandably, it makes many leaders uncomfortable, especially leaders who are up to chicanery and mischief with regard to the Faith. So this surreal posture is adopted by some of them.

On the one hand, they're working diligently to undermine and refashion the Faith, and on the other they still rely on the old idea of secrecy and closed-mouthedness behind which to hide. They keep what they can from the old way of doing business so they can totally remake the Church according to their ideas. They hide behind the bureaucracy to dismantle it. It's a strange thing. They insist on privacy and dress it all up in Church-speak, while they are simultaneously working actively against the Church.

It's akin to the idea that they always want the laity being more involved—until the laity actually *do* get involved, and then they freeze them out. What they should say is: "We want liberal, poorly formed, negligently educated Catholic laity involved, not faithful Catholic laity." It must be quite the quandary for many of these men who have made careers out of undermining the Faith by hiding *inside* the Faith now to encounter lay Catholics (with many victimized clerics quietly cheering them on) who are mad as Hell and aren't going to take it anymore.

Prelates don't get to run the Church like it's their private candy store. Crooked and deceitful clergy should no longer expect that they can just dismiss faithful Catholics who want answers to a host of questions. Some of those questions involve advancing a politically liberal agenda under the guise of fighting poverty, wrecking the liturgy under the guise of being more meaningful and participatory for the laity and so forth.

The Catholic free press has arrived and is ready to get down to business. The whole reason a free press exists in the secular world is to be a watchdog on government leaders. That idea translated into the Church is so totally foreign to many prelates and clerics that they don't even know how to process it. It's always been the case that they ran the show, were essentially accountable to no one, and did pretty much whatever they pleased.

Those days are fading away. As the Church continues to get smaller and grow more irrelevant in an increasingly hostile world, bishops are going to have to depend more and more on the few remaining faithful that exist. And those faithful want to know what's going on and are demanding accountability. After all, an excellent case can be made that it was the absence of a free press that allowed bad bishops to get the Church into this mess to begin with.

What Kind of America?
Originally aired September 28, 2015

H EY, CATHOLICS! What kind of America do you want? One polluted with the filth of dead babies and their pieces being sold and sodomite marriage and contraception taught to children and no-fault divorce and single-parent households and fatherless children and . . . shall we go on?

Then *wake up*. The famous Catholic author and thinker Hilaire Belloc once said, "You will not remedy the world until you have converted the world." And that about sums up the whole issue.

The question we have to consider is no less than this: Do we want to convert the culture to the holy Catholic faith, or do we want to fight a series of losing battles dying on the hills of abortion, gay marriage, sex ed in the schools, and so forth? The Catholic argument in those areas cannot be made because it cannot be *heard*. It cannot be heard because those making it are already, willfully or not, prejudiced against it.

They (and this sadly includes many former Catholics) have been swept up in a protestant-minded culture of thousands of denominations of which just about the only thing they can agree on is their animosity toward the Church of Rome. That Protestantism of yesteryear has predictably devolved into a mish-mash of indifferentism and secularism. Never forget, it was Protestantism that first, back in 1930, accepted and promoted contraception—and contraception has been the key to unlocking a culture built on sexual gratification.

The stinking heresy of Protestantism enjoys the second, most abundant portion of blame for the tailspin into evil in which the world finds itself. But it is Catholics who have failed to oppose this filthy heresy who will be judged the most harshly—and among them, the clergy themselves who have coddled this theological leviathan.

It all boils down to this: The Church is not like any other of these false religions. They are man-made. The Church is God-made. So those in the Church of God must distinguish themselves from the churches of man. Even on those spotty occasions when we might find some temporary common cause, it is always only temporary.

So Church leaders keep trying to find common ground with fellow Christians on admittedly shared issues of morality, like abortion and sodomy, but in the end, these efforts keep being subsumed into a maelstrom of political activity: Vote for the GOP, back this candidate. But Catholics, unlike their Protestant pals, can never make politics the first course of action. Protestants are at home in that arena because their fight has always been about winning the culture, and politics is a means to do that. But authentic Catholics have always understood, as Belloc said, *You fix the world by converting it to Catholicism.*

Think for a moment about the millions upon tens of millions of hours over the years that well-meaning but nonetheless protestant-influenced Catholics have spent on the abortion crusade. What would be the case today if instead, an equal number of hours had been spent trying to convert otherwise well-meaning allies to the One True Faith?

This isn't to say not to try and save the lives of babies from wicked abortionists, but to raise the question (which needs raising): How many spiritual compromises have been made along theological lines to end abortion? How many Catholic leaders have side-stepped those delicate questions about theology to advance the cause of the pro-life movement?

When that happens, the truth is not served. Truth denied is truth murdered. Catholics cannot confuse the mission, the mandate of the Church, with any other movement, cause, or allegiance, no matter how noble. Same with the issue of same-sex "marriage"; same with the death penalty; same with social justice, and on and on. The only thing the Church can be concerned with is *saving souls by converting them.*

Back in the 1960s and '70s, American Catholics had a choice either to fight for the Faith or fight for cultural causes, noble causes. They chose to fight for causes, failing to see that if they had fought for the Faith, they would have won over all the causes as a result. This happened for two major reasons: (1) the horror of children being murdered was blatantly obvious that it was easy to rally around; and (2) American Catholics had been taught, as a result of growing up in protestant America, to muffle their Catholic identity, to shut up and fit in. In the world of political conservatism, this meant leaving your overt Catholicism at the door when engaging in cultural issues.

That's why the bishops of the United States are fighting a ridiculous battle over the question of religious liberty—another losing proposition right out of the gate because the goal of it is not to convert, but to have the courts declare that we Catholics have the right to be left alone in our isolated, shrinking world. The reason bishops are happy to fight this way is to get as many people as possible together, united behind one cause so as to change the culture. But what many Catholics failed to see was that you cannot fight these single-issue battles and hope to win. You don't change the culture by fighting one battle at a time. You fight the culture by converting it.

You must fight huge-scale war in a huge-scale fashion, along a broad, sweeping front, not one, little, set-piece battle at a time. All we have done, been reduced to after nearly fifty years of culture wars, is one major defeat after another: no-fault divorce, rampant promiscuity, contraception, cohabitation, abortion, homosexual marriage . . .

Every single one of these used to be illegal. Why? Because most of America, without realizing it, *did* accept Catholic morality. Then was the moment for the Church to strike a preliminary blow against the Culture of Death, to abort it, so to speak, before it could see the light of day. But American Catholics were too afraid—of their own identity, of upsetting the much-longed for "place at the table" with the protestant majority. They failed to understand, to recognize, that they needed at that moment to push for a Great Evangelization; *then* was the moment for the New Evangelization.

Because protestant America was already half-listening to Catholic teachings and even living them, they might very well have been open to hearing, accepting, and converting to the other half, as demonstrated by Abp. Fulton Sheen's great push in 1950s television. But two generations later, that's no longer possible. Now the Church faces an impossible task, humanly speaking. What it could not do with its words and actions in the 1950s it must now do with its blood in the 2020s.

What kind of America do you want, my fellow Catholics? A never-ending set of skirmishes being lost on a cultural level, or a converted Catholic America? You can rest assured which one Heaven wants.

The Investment Game
Originally aired December 1, 2015

W HEN THE CATHOLIC LEAGUE'S Bill Donohue lashed out at Church Militant in 2015, calling us "right-wing nut jobs," understand what's going on. It's not personal, and neither, for the record, is this commentary.

There are ideologies at war here, just as in politics, but the stakes here are much higher than who wins the White House or a given U.S. Senate seat. Here we are talking about eternal destinies of millions of people—and that's what this is all about, and it's *all* this is about.

Donohue was responding in attack-dog mode—meaning slandering and defaming—because Church Militant had reported on the modernist Cdl. Donald Wuerl's limousine-liberal hypocrisy. Wuerl has lived in luxurious surroundings since practically the day of his priestly ordination and has run in the hoity-toity crowd of the Church Establishment ever since. If there were ever a prelate on the American scene who fits the description "born with a silver fork in his mouth," it would be His Eminence.

And what has he done with his influence? Maligned good prelates, waged the politics of personal destruction behind the scenes, distorted canon law on the matter of Holy Communion for Catholic politicians in favor of child murder, practically excused the sin of sodomy, and led the charge for sacrilegious reception of Holy Communion for adulterers, and on and on. This is a man Bill Donohue supports and cheers and protects.

So when he comes rushing to his aid and attacking those, like us, reporting on these facts, we ask questions like: Who is Bill Donohue? What is this apparent one-man show called the Catholic League? Where does it get its money? What does it do with its money? Why does he enjoy such support among the hierarchy that a man so crude would have their blessing to use the name "Catholic"?

He is, after all, rude, divisive, mean-spirited, judgmental, controversial—every trait the ruling class pretends to abhor, and yet, here they are, all of them, rolled up in one man who has carte blanche to say the crudest things. So since Mr. Donohue opened himself up, we went exploring and found out things that may cause some of the holier-than-Establishment types to back away.

For example, the Catholic League has two main sources of revenue each year: small-time, "rank and file" donations, and interest off a $35,000,000 investment fund. More on the group this money is invested with later, but here's a hint: It ain't all that Catholic and is going to be a little embarrassing for the supposedly "Catholic" League.

But first the cash flow: In 2013, the Catholic League had income from donations of about $2.7 million. It had expenses of about $2.83 million the same year. Included in those expenses were Bill Donohue's inflated salary and benefits of close to a half million: nearly $500,000. So, including Bill's pay, Catholic League would have shown a net loss of $130,000 in 2013. And it would have been a loss except for the $482,000 in interest income from that $35,000,000 investment fund.

No interest income each year to shore up its negative cash flow and Catholic League is going down the drain—unless, of course, Bill gives back a hefty portion of his half million. So Catholic League is essentially a break even or losing proposition each year, whose near-lone ranger is paid from a huge investment fund to keep the ship from sinking. So the spotlight needs to turn to that investment fund whose interest dividend is critical to the Catholic League's survival.

Who is the investment fund? What do you know—it's the Establishment Church's goldmine: Christian Brothers Investment Services (CBIS), the largest investor of Catholic money in the world, counting among its clients archdioceses, religious institutes, educational organizations, charities, and, of course, the Catholic League. And how does CBIS invest all this Catholic money? A very fair question. You would think it's investing in businesses and causes not involved in anything immoral or contributing to the culture of evil, right?

On their website, they do say something like that, claiming they refuse to invest in companies involved, for example, in weapons. Fine. But what about pornography? After all, the U.S. bishops, many of whose dioceses are investors with CBIS, just issued a statement decrying pornography. CBIS is pretty clear in that regard as well: CBIS will not invest in companies that produce pornography. Good for them.

But they suddenly dismount the high horse when it comes to investing in companies that *distribute pornography*. Crack open that portfolio and you see Google, Time-Warner, Comcast—all corporate giants involved in the distribution of porn. So CBIS takes a principled stand in not investing in the studio where pornography is produced, but are all in on the companies that bring it to your computer screens and TVs. There are other giant organizations in their portfolio who represent the honor guard in the roll call of the culture of death, supporting abortion, contraception, sodomite marriage—just go down the list: Amazon, Microsoft, HP, and so forth. You get the idea.

Now, to be sure, Catholic League isn't the only one invested in this stuff. We'll be examining many others in the coming days. But they are the one that bills itself the slugger in the street, the fighter for Catholic rights and all that. So how does this work exactly?

The leader, Catholic Establishment water-bot Bill Donohue, sucks half a million a year out of an organization that loses money—losses, except for the income earned by investments in a Catholic investment group that invests in giant Culture-of-Death and Culture-of-Evil companies—the same companies that back, bankroll, and advance policies and laws that Donohue fights against?

Wow! Now that's quite the racket. Earn a living off the lucre earned by investing in your enemy's activities, and fund your activities by asking for donations to fight against the evil that your enemies promote. Now that is quite the business plan, Mr. Donohue.

You make a half million a year. Catholic League is kept afloat by interest from immoral investments. And you attack and defame faithful Catholics who shine a spotlight on the evils in the Church, all the while giving the pro-gay crowd a pass on the St. Patrick's Day parade. No wonder Catholic League is the go-to attack dog for the Establishment crowd. They all understand one another so well. The Establishment is kept afloat by money by fellow Catholics—*your money*—the constant appeals to your wallet to help with this cause and help with that cause.

I even received my annual appeal from Notre Dame. It hit the trash. And that's what you have to do. Remember, this garbage has been flying largely under the radar for fifty-plus years, operating in quiet, putting on a Catholic face when it needs to and advising evil, intentionally or not.

Want to know how to get a good resistance going? Turn off the money supply—to the bishops' social justice causes, to Church bodies and outfits that invest in some of America's most pro-Culture-of-Death companies, and to nonprofits that have the blessings of the Establishment.

This shell game has gone on long enough.

What the Vote Means
Originally aired February 3, 2016

TWO HEADLINES COMING OUT of the Iowa caucuses: the evangelical vote was 68 percent of the Republican vote; the Catholic vote was 16 percent. The Catholic vote was what you would expect because that's the proportion of Catholics in the state of Iowa.

Interestingly, though, the evangelical vote was split almost evenly among the top three Republican vote-getters: Ted Cruz the winner, Donald Trump, and Marco Rubio—the last two essentially tied for second. Typically, what happens in Iowa has very little influence in New Hampshire. But as Church Militant reported, Cruz has been heavily courting the smaller evangelical vote in New Hampshire, and that might be enough to influence the final outcome.

But the real headline, and something all comfortable Establishment types should pay close attention to: The anti-Establishment candidates in each party won; the Establishment pols got hammered.

Bernie Sanders shouldn't have been anywhere *near* Hillary. Yet from the beginning of his campaign, he portrayed himself as the anti-Establishment guy, as did Cruz and Trump and Ben Carson on the GOP side. If you add together their final votes, you get almost two out of every three Republican votes cast.

All the Establishment candidates on each side were feeling pretty good in the beginning. As time went by, the big boys started getting more and more concerned. The Establishment candidates had all the support, experience, endorsements, and money. Jeb Bush, in fact, spent $65 million to come in sixth place with a miserable three percent.

When you consider the outcomes coupled with the turnout in record numbers for each party, it's clear a lot of people are dissatisfied across the board. The reasons are varied, but what is certain is that those in power, both in politics and other arenas, are no longer trusted, or at best viewed with deep suspicion.

The concern should not be limited to politicians. Trust in clergy is at an all-time low at 45 percent. That has plummeted from a high of 67 percent just thirty years ago. Think about that for a moment: Two out of three Americans trusted the clergy a generation ago. Now it's less than one in two. And much of that is owing to the homosexual priest sex abuse scandal.

But even among faithful Catholics, the rate of frustration is increasing. The non-stop flow of scandalous stories from seemingly every diocese continues to erode the trust and confidence of the remaining faithful. What Washington, D.C. and the U.S. bishops seem to have in common is a tone-deafness, an ivory-tower attitude expressed toward those beneath them. It cannot be this way in the Church.

What does the vote mean? It shows a huge level of frustra-tion—and anyone who thinks that frustration is confined to just politics has missed the point entirely. Each side, the liberals and the conservatives, are doubling down, wanting their respective leaders to harden their position and leader-ship, to advance their respective orthodoxies. There is no more room in the middle. Each side's supporters are fed up with their Establishments and want authentic leadership.

If the faithful bishops of the United States can see this and respond accordingly, there might be hope to restore a robust Catholic Church, but they have got to give up the "big tent" Catholicism once and for all.

This election is proving that Establishment types are being given their final notice. Love your sheep, or you will lose them.

Not What It Looks Like
Originally aired July 28, 2016

A S FAITHFUL CATHOLICS—as opposed to just cultural or lapsed Catholics—watch in horror as Hillary Clinton moves one step closer to her life ambition of being president, a natural tendency arises to become a default Republican supporter.

Hillary Clinton's worldview is evil. The woman is possessed by an evil view of the world. She is a danger to everyone she is around because of her insidiousness and deceit. Under no circumstances can she ever be supported by anyone Catholic. Let's just get that out of the way right up front. She is a living, walking, talking embodiment of an enemy of Christ.

That said, the default option of supporting the Republican Party, candidate, and agenda is not as clear cut as many may think. This is not your father's GOP. Case in point: the presence of Peter Thiel, openly gay founder of PayPal and early investor in Facebook, at the 2016 GOP convention in Cleveland, Ohio. During his speech, he proudly proclaimed his homosexuality to the audience—which reacted with wild applause.

That speech was a watershed moment for the GOP. Despite all the hoopla about how pro-life the party platform is, the truth is that the platform carries no weight at all and is merely symbolic—and those who put it together are among the most elite and hardworking grassroots types that are given a bit of a reward for all their efforts during the year.

The reality in the GOP these days is what you heard when Thiel announced he was proud to be gay and a Republican. The moral issues as issues have long since been abandoned by the party leadership. The horse is out of the barn. The train has pulled out of the station. That ship has sailed. Use whatever analogy you want. The party as a party will never again be rolling back to pre-same-sex marriage days or pre-*Roe v. Wade* days.

The GOP has moved beyond these issues because the party leadership has correctly recognized that the American people don't really care about these issues. That's why we still have abortion. That's why the Supreme Court in 2015 could comfortably hand down its same-sex marriage ruling, with barely a whimper from anyone. America has become an immoral country, at relative ease with Her immorality. Contraception led the way, then abortion, then no-fault divorce, then same-sex marriage—evil multiplying evil.

And America will pay for Her immoralities. Some of the punishment has already come in a deepening economic crisis, the loss of material goods, the psychological and emotional impact of devastated families, and so on. But these will pale in comparison to the final blow. The Roman Empire went on a slow, steady decline and blew up at the end.

America's decline is steady, but because of technology, it will not be slow. And like many empires before ours, America will also blow up. The Democrats push evil, and for now, the Republicans stand silent about the evil. But more and more, the GOP is coming on board with the evil. The GOP is not what it looks like; it's not your father's Republican Party—but many political conservatives have yet to wake up to this reality.

In the 1960s and early '70s, the Democratic Party under-went a profound shift in principles, but huge numbers of Democratic voters didn't realize it until too late. The foundational shift was summed up in former Democrat Ronald Reagan's famous 1962 comment, "I didn't leave the Democratic Party. The Party left me."

Well, the same thing is happening now to the Republican Party and Republican voters. The party is moving; the move is almost complete—not quite, but almost—from the pro-life, pro-family party to the party barely distinguishable from the Democrats on the issues of evil. This shift needs to be greatly considered by faithful Catholics.

Many faithful Catholics have spent years working hard for various candidates and ballot initiatives and referenda to keep society as moral as possible. Face the music here: *We've lost.* And Our Blessed Lord may very well be sending us a message. We have for too long with a sincere heart put our trust in princes. Bad move. We should have been evangelizing instead.

If a majority of the electorate had been converted to authentic Catholicism, we wouldn't be in this mess we are now in and from which there is no natural escape. But we didn't do that. We didn't feel the need to try and convert a protestant nation with the seeds of its own destruction ever present. Church leaders were content to do little, as evi-denced by the shocking lack of conversions *before* Vatican II.

We Catholics sat back, watched the world go by, didn't care enough for souls, and as a result, now have to face the reality that the souls of our loved ones are threatened. Even still, we hear various religious leaders, like their forebears, keeping silent, ignoring the coming storm, even pretending there is nothing to be concerned about by declaring we have a reasonable hope that all men are saved.

Even among faithful Catholics who are politically involved is there a conscious, honest-to-God awareness that what is really being fought over here is not constitutional principles but the reality that the more corrupt society becomes, the more souls will be damned. Catholics have not devoted enough of their time to converting the culture. We have spent too much time trying to effect natural change through the political realm.

The kingdom to which we belong is not of this world. We are called to convert people to the truth of Jesus Christ in His Holy, Catholic, Apostolic Church founded on Blessed Peter. If people believed and lived Catholic truth, there would be none of these evils. Yet we missed our window.

Catholics' duty is to save souls. You cannot save souls without also having an impact for the good on the natural order, because the supernatural plane is higher. Effect good on the supernatural level, and it will, to borrow a phrase from Ronald Reagan's days, "trickle down" to the natural order—trickle-down spirituality, as it were.

But the leaders—the bishops and religious superiors—have not followed this path. They have not instructed the laity to follow this path. And what do we now see? One major party already completely controlled by the diabolical, and the other major party in the process of also being controlled by him.

Catholic pro-lifers should have been at least as concerned with the souls of the protestant pro-lifers praying with them at the abortion mills as they were with abortion itself. Did the conversation come up that we should go back to the days when contraception was illegal? Was the discussion ever had that all religions are not the same, that there is only one true Faith?

You cannot effect change on the natural level that will have any lasting effect if you forsake the supernatural. The GOP is no longer what it looks like, and America is no longer the country it used to be.

Chapter Six

Hell

FOR THE PAST THIRTY YEARS, perhaps longer, the prevailing attitude in education has been to deny that there are consequences to doing poorly. The aim has been to protect, many would say coddle, youngsters and shield them from the harsh reality that is life.

No matter how noble (or foolhardy) the motive that began this mindset, what has emerged in its wake is a generation or two of people who feel (with emphasis on *feel* because there is no thought involved) they are entitled to win, advance, be promoted, and that bad actions have no bad consequences. Everyone gets a participation trophy because the worst thing that can happen is that little Johnny have his feelings hurt. God forbid he actually be inspired to do better and apply himself for the next contest.

This "participation trophy" thought has invaded the Church. In fact, it may very well be the case that it began in the Church, as pastors, bishops, and religious just stopped talking and preaching about Hell—the ultimate consequence.

In theological terms, it's been considered enough to just show up on earth, to exist, and Heaven is automatically guaranteed. Perhaps not for the worst of the worst—maybe Hitler is in Hell—but God is so loving that He ignores our immoral choices and forgives us without our even needing to ask or think we need forgiving. It's a reward from the Almighty for just showing up. With God there are no lovely parting gifts because everyone's a winner.

Such is the folly of modern Churchmen as they seal their own fates, denying or downplaying the reality of the very thing from which the Son of God came to earth to save us.

Society of the Damned
Originally aired July 21, 2011

A S WE LOOK AROUND THE SITUATION in the Church today, there is one major missing ingredient: a firm belief in and acceptance of the Church's dogmatic teaching on Hell. It is simply dismissed.

But consider this: the moment of Judgment, that moment when the soul of an individual about to be damned as a result of his own choices, not God's, comes into the presence of Almighty God at the moment of death. To that soul, the loving face of Our Blessed Lord, Whose Sacred Heart burns with a passion for their salvation, appears to them to be a horror, a terrible fright, a countenance of unbearable ugliness Whose presence they cannot bear. They curse and desire nothing more than to be as far away as possible from His loving face. If they could, they would strike out and hit His face and spit on Him as the Roman soldiers did when they jammed the crown of thorns into His scalp.

Whatever indifference or disregard they had for God this side of death is now dramatically elevated to an intense hatred, a bitter, foul disgust of being in the Divine Presence. So they flee from Him and rapidly join themselves in community to the society of the damned, forever, where with full knowledge they realize that for all eternity their lot is damnation and never-ending misery.

When Catholics lose sight of this one fact, when they disregard the actual reason for our existence, when they lightly shrug off that every soul will come to the seat of judgment and Scripture tells us many will share this fate—when Catholics forget this, they have lost their way and their ability to lead others to Heaven. This is the entire reason for the Church's existence: to prevent souls from joining the society of the damned, helping them to join instead the heavenly city.

But there are too many in the Church these days who never seem to give this ultimate reality a thought. The seemingly constant stress on the affairs of this world, as though it will last forever, is sorely misplaced. No matter what sort of Heaven on earth is established through cooperation with worldly authorities, abandoning this truth in practice will not end well. The Church's mission is to preach the truth so that those who hear and accept the truth will live in that truth and light for eternity. In so many quarters of the Church today, this doesn't even appear on the radar.

There is too much emphasis on parish closings and fundraising issues and cooperation with forces indifferent to or even hostile to the Church. So many leaders and those in positions of authority, clerical and lay alike, are so focused on keeping the bureaucracy running that they have lost all sense of mission regarding why the bureaucracy has been established. The Establishment should be at the service of the Bride of Christ—not the other way around.

Until more come to their senses, the crisis will only deepen. And that means, in these current days, all we can pray is that these souls are somehow saved—although exactly how that could happen remains a mystery, considering so many of them live earthly lives divorced from their Heavenly Father.

If the Establishment Church doesn't preach the realities of the next life, how can we possibly expect that these people divorced from God here will suddenly do an about-face at the judgment seat and out of nowhere decide they now want to live with God? When Church leaders fail in their mission, it seems logical to conclude the society of the damned increases.

A Bishop in Hell
Originally aired June 6, 2013

O UR BLESSED LORD ESTABLISHED HIS CHURCH so that the responsibility for it would lay in the hands of the Apostles and their successors: the bishops. They have all the responsibility, which is why they have all the authority. The laity have no real authority in the Church; whatever some laity may possess comes to them from the good graces of their bishop.

Because all the responsibility for teaching and governing rests with the bishops, they are the ones in greatest peril of their souls. They are the leaders, and because of that simple fact, they are judged by an entirely different standard. A leader does not get judged by the same standard as the rank and file. Imagine the absurdity of giving a man all the power but none of the responsibility for the consequences of his decisions.

For this reason, when one looks around the Church these days, is it really an unreasonable question to ask: Could many of the bishops be on the road to Hell? This question is asked in all charity for their salvation. Think about it: In America alone more than half of Catholics have left the Church—more than 30 million. Of those still technically in the Church, many ignore the Church's teachings on everyday issues or morality, deny one or more dogmas of the Faith, like the Real Presence or the superiority of the Catholic faith.

True, it was not today's bishops who set these wheels in motion. Many of them were just simple seminarians when all this madness began, and they were schooled in it. But while they didn't set these wheels in motion, many of them have kept them rolling. They allow dissident speakers to speak on church property; they allow dissenters to get awards and honors; they seek after a distorted view of ecumenism; they marginalize or silence orthodox priests; they allow liberal priests to remain in charge of parishes (priests whom they know are not being faithful to the magisterial teachings and are leading souls into confusion and indifference); they will not speak at length on the spiritual realities like sin and Hell and the devil, but pay lobbyists to promote public policy on immigration and the environment and gun control and the canard of religious freedom.

Rarely if ever do you hear a bishop talk about souls going to Hell. Rarely if ever do you hear a bishop denouncing and decrying contraception. You could wait a month of Sundays before you will hear a bishop say that the Catholic Church and only the Catholic Church was established by Jesus Christ and is the One True Faith. Too many of them speak in half-truths, duck the hard issues, hide behind labels of charity and prudence, ignore the reality and consequences of their cowardice and rebellion, and sit back and watch the destruction continue to implode the Church.

Only these men have the authority to begin to reverse this destruction. They can purge the disloyal priests from their charge, take charge of the education system in their diocese by firing teachers and administrators who will not adhere to the teachings of the Church, they can by the stroke of a pen begin to end the flood of liturgical abuses at parish Masses each week. There is so much they can do, and their refusal to do any of it does not bode well for them when they come before the throne of Jesus Christ. How can it? He has given them charge to tend to His sheep, not their sheep. And what do they allow? They allow the wolves free access in the classrooms, pulpits, seminaries, RCIA classes, etc.

Their power is singular: to protect the sheep. If they fail to do this, what else would common sense dictate other than their own damnation?

Think for a moment of the terrible scene of a bishop who dies, who in this life was popular in the eyes of man for something other than his holiness. He placed his ambitions above the will of God and sought after the praise of men and would not challenge them by announcing the hard sayings of Our Lord. And here he now stands before the throne of God, his soul bare, naked in the glaring light of Truth. Judgment is passed on him that he is damned, and just before he descends into the pit, he is shown all those souls who on his watch were damned because of his lack of love for them.

It will no longer matter that he was a cardinal or bishop for whom people often spoke a good word. The words he will now hear for all eternity will be the curses of those who perished on his watch because he did nothing to save them. As they tear him to shreds, they will throw in his face the mockery of his attempts to please men with talk of immigration reform and social justice and gun control and a host of other earthly measures that will be burned up in the fires of Hell. He will forever be a slave of the demons, who will have special tortures reserved for the heirs of the Apostles. The pains of the damned are beyond description for the lowliest of the baptized; imagine what they are like for those exalted with the fullness of the priesthood.

Would a good bishop who has the courage to declare war on the unfaithful in his diocese and in his own chancery be crucified by those same unfaithful men and women? Without a doubt. The bishop's persecution at the hands of the liberal, modernist Establishment might often seem unbearable. But in suffering for the Faith, he will save his soul and the souls of many others. This is the rule for every Catholic bishop and layman. But for the bishop, failing to do this holds a special torture in the dungeons and prisons of Hell precisely because so many others are there *because of his actions* (and inaction).

The pains of Hell are beyond compare. Saint Augustine once said that the fires of Hell are so intense that trying to understand them in relation to the fires of earth would be like trying to understand the pain of earthly fire by looking at a painting of fire. It would only make sense that the pain a bishop would suffer in Hell would be among the worst because of his noble standing on earth. Catholics must pray and fast for the bishops, that they might be strong shepherds, and in the process be preserved from eternal damnation.

Do Non-Catholics Go to Hell?
Originally aired April 24, 2015

D O ALL NON-CATHOLICS GO TO HELL? It's a question that's been the subject of many heated conversations.

There is a deeper question here, because there is a deeper principle involved. The deeper principle beyond being a "card-carrying, on the parish rolls" Catholic is: How does one actually attain salvation? What is necessary for salvation? What is necessary to get to Heaven? That's the more fundamental question, the foundation from which springs the further question about being in the Catholic Church.

The Church teaches that one must be in a state of grace upon death to achieve salvation. And a person can only be in a state of grace or in a state of mortal sin. If a person dies in a state of unrepented mortal sin, he descends immediately and directly into Hell for all eternity, where he suffers the tortures of his demonic masters, but is most tortured from his everlasting separation from God, Whom he knows he was created to be with and yet detests at the same time.

So the primary question is: How does a person achieve a state of grace? A state of grace is the state where the life of the Blessed Trinity is present in the soul. Sanctifying grace comes to the soul from the first moment in baptism and helps to sustain the supernatural virtues: the theological virtues of faith, hope, and charity. A man dying without these virtues dies without God. He is owned by Hell.

It is impossible to possess supernatural hope and supernatural charity in combination with supernatural faith without sanctifying grace. Mortal sin ("mortal" coming from the Latin *morte*, or "death") means the supernatural life of the soul is now gone. The soul is dead spiritually. For a while it possesses its natural aspect of giving life to the body, animating the flesh—but when the end comes, not only is the body dead, but the soul remains in a perpetual state of death: the Second Death of which the Scriptures speak. Its now everlasting pain is to have to endure death when it was created for divine life.

How to avoid this worst of realities is to die not in a state of deadly sin but in a state of life, divine life. Our Blessed Lord points the way most vividly and lovingly: "If a man loves me, he will keep my word, and my Father will love him, and we will come to him and make our home with him" (John 14:23). This is the most direct way to understand what is meant by a state of grace: that the Holy Trinity takes up residence in our souls. God lives in us; we are in a perpetual state of possessing divine grace, divine life. The only thing that can alter this most precious of all realities is to commit mortal sin. When that happens, God immediately flees, for He cannot abide sin. It is an abomination to Him. Purity cannot abide that which is impure.

So the key to the question "Is there salvation outside the Church?" is to first understand that the Church's role is to assist souls in attaining and maintaining a state of grace. This is the sole purpose for the sacraments: to infuse supernatural grace into the soul, visible signs instituted by Our Lord for the imparting of grace.

Now it's true, God's grace is not bound by the sacraments. He can certainly operate outside of them. He did in such manifest cases as the conversion of St. Paul, for example. Saul received a singular grace of conversion. And while that grace was not mediated through a formal sacrament, it nevertheless did come through the Church, as all graces do. It was, after all, the Church that was praying non-stop for relief from the murderous Saul. In answer to the prayer of the Church about Saul, God sent them Paul.

The purpose of the Church in the grand scheme is to create saints, to make us holy. As St. Peter tells us, "But you are a chosen race, a royal priesthood, a holy nation" (1 Peter 2:9). When he wrote his first letter, the first pope was speaking to the first Catholics. We Catholics sometimes forget this truth, owing to the protestant co-opting of the Scriptures as though they belonged to them. They most certainly do not. They never have.

The Bible, the canon of Scripture, is Catholic, period. So the formula laid out for us in Scripture has specific and singular reference to those souls alive within the body of Christ—His Catholic Church. When Catholic souls plunge into spiritual death through committing mortal sin, they have a sacramental remedy to be resurrected: the sacrament of confession. But when a non-Catholic soul, even one baptized in some protestant denomination, falls into mortal sin, what remedy does it possess? Short of an act of perfect contrition prior to death—nothing. Such a man dies in his mortal sin.

The debate over salvation outside the Church is kind of a moot question, then, as it's generally argued. The example case is always brought up: Does the "good" protestant husband and father go to Hell because he wasn't Catholic? That question is framed totally incorrectly. It should not be asked, "Will he go to Heaven if he wasn't Catholic?" but rather: "Was he in a state of grace—and if he wasn't Catholic, how was it possible for him to be in a state of grace?"

We can never know with certitude, of course, the disposition of any particular soul; that is completely in the realm of Our Lord as Judge. But in the hypothetical discussions in which people engage, we can ask these questions. We speak in hypotheticals because principles of understanding fall from them. And the singular principle that falls from all of this is: It is much more difficult to be saved if you are not a Catholic with access to the sacraments to restore you to and keep you in a state of grace. Faithful, sacrament-frequenting Catholics are much more likely to be saved than anyone else because such a man is much more likely to die in a state of grace— which is necessary to be saved.

This is the whole point of evangelizing: to help people understand the perilous risk to which they are exposing their souls if they do not become Catholic and faithfully receive the sacraments given to us by Our Lord Himself for our salvation. All salvation comes through the Catholic Church, and outside of Her there is no salvation.

The Judas Question
Originally aired April 28, 2015

JUDAS ISCARIOT IS IN HELL. That's the unanimous opinion of the saints, Fathers and Doctors of the Church. It is the continuing witness of the greatest minds of the Church.

There is a current of thought running through many contemporary Catholic circles that seeks to rehabilitate Judas, to give the impression that he was saved. And the reason is somewhat duplicitous: It isn't so much to raise up Judas as to downplay their sin.

The unconscious thinking goes something like: "If Judas were saved, then I'm not so bad off." *Much* hangs on and surrounds this whole topic of Judas' damnation. For example, Swiss theologian Hans Urs von Balthasar was more than anxious to rationalize that Judas is *not* damned so von Balthasar could promote the nutty idea that "we have a reasonable hope that all men are saved." He even wrote a book by that title, and the question of Judas looms large.

Popular bishop Robert Barron has openly dismissed and shoved aside the writing of Church Fathers and Doctors like St. Augustine and St. Thomas Aquinas and thrown his lot in with von Balthasar, publicly declaring that he thinks the saints are wrong and von Balthasar is right.

For von Balthasar's strange idea of having a reasonable hope that everyone is saved, he needs to paint the picture that Judas is saved. Judas *wasn't* saved, though. So von Balthasar's "theology" on this score falls flat on its face—and so too then does Bp. Barron's proclamations and the whole Church of Nice approach to sin and Hell.

And what the great minds of the Church are unanimous on about the damnation of Judas isn't that he betrayed Our Lord. Rather, it was that he added to that sin by committing suicide, denying the mercy of God. They note that he was remorseful and then despaired, and *that* was what sealed his damnation.

Here is what some of them had to say:

"For Judas, when he killed himself, killed a wicked man, and passed from this life chargeable not only with the death of Christ, but also with his own: for though he killed himself on account of his crime, his killing himself was another crime." ~St. Augustine

"In the case of Judas, the abuse of grace was the reason for his reprobation, since he was made reprobate because he died without grace." ~St. Thomas Aquinas

"The godless betrayer, shutting his mind to all these things [offerings of God's mercy], turned upon himself, not with a mind to repent, but in the madness of self-destruction: so that this man who had sold the Author of life to the executioners of His death, even in the act of dying, sinned unto the increase of his own eternal punishment." ~Pope St. Leo the Great

There are many others we could bring forth, but the point is made. There has never been any serious consideration in the 2,000-year history of the Church that Judas is anything other than damned.

Why is this so important today? Because there is an attempt to sidestep this issue, to rehabilitate Judas (or at least ignore him) as the fake mercy march is on among progressives and liberals in the Church to reduce Hell to a fantasy, or just something you have to hold out as a "real possibility," but not something you have to take seriously.

The point is: If Judas is damned, then what von Balthasar (and by extension Bp. Barron) likes to throw out there for your consideration or to confuse you—that "we have a reasonable hope that all men are saved"—simply *cannot* be true.

If Judas is damned, then there can be *no* hope, reasonable or otherwise, that "all men are saved," because here is at least one who wasn't. And if *one* can be damned, a whole hell of a lot more can be as well—and *that* is where the Church of Nice does not and cannot go.

Hell is not just a real "possibility." *It is real*—and people go there.

The Four Last Things
Originally aired February 10, 2016

NO CROSS, NO SALVATION. Or, as Ven. Abp. Fulton Sheen used to put it, "There can be no Easter Sunday without first a Good Friday."

A focal point of Lent has always been what the Church calls the Four Last Things, originally in Greek *eschaton*. There is a whole field of understanding dedicated to the Four Last Things. It's called eschatology.

What are the Four Last Things? Death, judgment, Heaven, and Hell. And by "Last," Holy Mother Church proposes that nothing comes after them. We will each die, undergo judgment, and go to Heaven or Hell. And that will be that. Game over.

Now, on Ash Wednesday in parishes and dioceses where the reality of the eschaton is taken seriously, when the ashes are administered, you are likely to hear the words "Remember, man, that thou art dust, and unto dust you shall return." That is a focused statement coming from your Mother to snap you to, even if brusquely.

In parishes and dioceses where the eschaton isn't taken seriously because we supposedly have a reasonable hope that all men are saved, dying is just passing over, judgment is no big deal, and Hell doesn't exist for anyone except Genghis Khan and Hitler, you are much more likely to hear the watered-down "Repent and believe the Good News." Yay! It's so fun in Catholic lollipop land.

What that sad-sack expression of theology fails to make clear is the sober message that death is stalking you and ready to snatch you up to the judgment throne of God. Every day, 150,000 people leave earth forever—100 souls a minute. How many will stand before their God ill-equipped and unprepared to face the divine justice?

And what is justice? It's not God being a big meanie like the Church of Nice crowd likes to portray it. That is a strawman characterization of what the Church teaches. Holy Mother Church simply states that God will give a man what he deserves; that's what justice is.

The killer gets the chair; the speeder gets a fine. It would be unjust to treat them the same, because they aren't. Likewise, the living saint gets Heaven, the mortally sinful man gets Hell. Again, it would be unjust that they get treated the same because they aren't. And Sacred Scripture says, implies, indicates, and flat-out states in many passages: You get what you deserve based on your actions.

One glaring line: "For he will render to every man according to his works" (Romans 2:6). So much for the dumb, uninformed notion on the part of many Protestants that once they pronounce on the name of the Lord Jesus, they are saved. They must have missed out on the day the class went over inconvenient Bible passages that say, "Not every one who says to me, 'Lord, Lord,' shall enter the kingdom of heaven, but he who does the will of my Father who is in heaven" (Matthew 7:21).

The reason the Church says "Remember, man, that thou art dust, and unto dust you shall return." is to snap you to attention. If there weren't some big deal about dying—because the judgment awaits immediately after it—then there wouldn't be the need to be warned about it.

The Church of Nice is uncomfortable about Ash Wednesday. It's why they changed the words. "Believe the Good News" is much easier emotionally and psychologically to cope with than "You're going to die and you'd better be ready or you're going to be damned." And the Church of Nice is all about emotion and psychology, right?

Heaven is the reward, what we are owed, in a sense—the sense being that Our Blessed Lord has promised it. "If a man loves me, he will keep my word, and my Father will love him, and we will come to him and make our home with him" (John 14:23).

The first pope warns us explicitly to be on the lookout for Satan, "a roaring lion, seeking someone to devour" (1 Peter 5:8). Be on your watch, therefore. Do not spend your Lent in some Church of Nice coma. For some of us, it will be our last Lent.

If Satan is trying to devour you, then the least you can do is put up some resistance, literally for the love of God, Who made you to be with *Him*—not to be cat food for the diabolical lion. Every minute, more than a hundred souls are brought to the judgment seat of Almighty God. How many do you suppose every minute now are in a state of grace, meaning not being in a state of mortal sin?

Is the drug dealer who gets shot in a drug deal gone bad?

How about the cheating wife killed in a car accident coming back from her rendezvous?

What about the priest who dies of a heart attack after giving counsel he knows contradicts Church teaching?

What about the abortionist content to pad his bank account with blood money, or the Catholic pro-abortion politician who keeps conditions legal for him to continue in business?

What about the bishop who suffers an aneurysm after having spent sixteen years allowing heresy and heterodoxy to spread throughout his diocese?

What about the young turk in the hook-up culture crowd who is killed by some random event?

What about the chancery official covering up scandal and damaging souls?

We are given lists of people in Sacred Scripture who will never see God in the face: cowards, liars, murderers, sorcerers, etc. Does anyone in their right mind really think for one minute that, with more than a hundred people dying every single minute, thousands dying an hour, every hour, 150,000 dying daily, every day, that all these people are going to Heaven?

The Church of Nice does—or rather, they simply don't let the discussion come up. They deflect. The point of Lent is to prevent the deflection and get down to reality. *I am going to die. You are going to die.* The only question is: Who first?

Lent is to remind us of death, so we can have eternal life. Death, judgment, Heaven, Hell—nothing else matters. Embrace the Cross.

Slouching into Hell
Originally aired March 3, 2016

M ANY OF US HAVE FAMILY and loved ones who are on
their way to Hell. Despite the load of garbage spewing
out of the Church of Nice that we have a reasonable hope that
all men are saved, we know deep down that there isn't a ring
of truth to that. We know that people do not go to Heaven
who are indifferent or lukewarm toward the Faith. Our
Blessed Lord Himself tells us He will vomit the lukewarm from
His mouth. The same is true of those hostile to the Faith; live
in opposition to the Holy Catholic Faith, and a person dies
forever in opposition to God. And this is true even if we love
the person. Our love for them does not cancel out their
indifference toward God.

The reality for many people is that their loved ones are not
directly hostile toward God. They don't walk around actively
cursing Him and carrying on with great drama. They simply
live lives of great indifference to God. It could be said they are
slouching into Hell. They are lazily, slothfully strolling along,
walking down a long and winding path—with emphasis on
down.

Many of you have spoken to your loved ones—children,
siblings, grandchildren—and no matter what you say, nothing
seems to get through. Not only is it frightening on a supernatural level, it's almost maddening on a natural level. Why
are they so unconcerned? Why won't they listen?

The bottom line is because they have rejected the grace of the
call to conversion. They more than likely care on some level,
but not enough to have remorse and then repent. And next to
nothing you say will engender a change—nothing you *say*, at
least. But something you *do* might bring about a change.

You must pray for something to crash into their lives and
awaken them to the supernatural peril into which they've
placed their souls. This isn't to say you need to pray for a
calamity to strike; but you should pray that whatever needs
to happen does happen—even if it seems on the surface bad.

However bad it may be, it will be nowhere near as bad as their eternal damnation. And this kind of prayer requires enormous strength on your part; it requires a sacrifice of great proportion.

In my own case, my mother, Anne, prayed for my brother Marshall and me: "Jesus, I don't care what you do to me. Do whatever you have to do, but spare the eternal lives of my two sons."

Doctors discovered the earliest stages of cancer in her stomach after she prayed that prayer. But it takes a spiritual Hercules to utter a prayer like that and *mean* it. The back story on that prayer was all the preceding years of prayer my mother made to get to a point, to arrive at a spiritual point of strength, where she could make that final prayer. For many years my mother had prayed for her two sons. She grew frustrated at Our Lord's apparent silence; she even scolded Him from time to time for not listening to her.

The point is: Even the one offering the sacrifice and prayers must themselves be prepared to offer an even more efficacious sacrifice. All those years, and what I'm certain were thousands of rosaries, were storing up in my mom a warehouse of graces, even though she had no personal "feeling" of it. She knew on some intellectual level that God would answer her prayers, but she seldom felt that way—which is another reason Catholics do not move on our emotions, but on our intellectual certitude.

And then one day, moved by grace, she threw up her hands and prayed the perfect sacrificial prayer: *I don't care about myself; use me to save them.*

She had crossed the spiritual Rubicon, and now her great sacrifice was ready, prepared by all those years of suffering in frustration and grumbling and irritation—and *love.* My mother was indeed a St. Monica, and this is what we must all pray to become on behalf of souls. It is not enough to pray for someone's salvation; we must pray that we can stand in their place and bear some of the cost of their sins. What is a sacrifice, after all, other than an exchange, where one thing is traded for another? Our Blessed Lord Himself showed us the way.

This kind of heroism is not usually available by just the simple asking. In my mother's case, she had to be prepared to come to this point of truly sacrificial prayer. We must pray to be brought to this point as well. We must not merely comprehend the power of sacrifice, we must desire to be sacrificed ourselves for the love of souls.

Never give up on your children's salvation. Never lose your hope. But do ask, pray to become a living sacrifice for souls—your loved ones, and others. While the Church was built on the blood of the martyrs, it is sustained through the sacrifices of each generation of martyrs—red martyrs and white martyrs. The Cross is the key, as it always has been.

Chapter Seven

Homosexuality in the Church

FOLLOWING VATICAN II, there was a sea change in the men who were flooding into seminary compared to previous generations: the homosexual. There were, of course, men with same-sex attraction who had been ordained in previous years, and scandals would sometimes emerge in parishes, seminaries, religious houses, monasteries. The writings and preachings of St. Peter Damien attest to this sad fact.

But the ascendancy and control, the power and influence exercised by this contingent of psychologically disturbed men is what is new. Consider how the scales tipped within the ordained class since the middle of the twentieth century. First there was the great exodus from the priesthood in the ten to fifteen years following the Second Vatican Council. Most of these men who left did so to get married; they forsook their vows. So the numbers and influence of heterosexual men declined. At the same time, that meant the number of men who were homosexual saw a corresponding increase, just through the desertion and attrition of non-homosexual seminarians.

Cliques and networks began forming and would extend their influence to even the most recent times. Once a decade or so had passed, homosexual seminarians became homosexual priests, who used their network and influence to promote and advance one another, eventually to positions of power on seminary staffs, where heterosexual or more orthodox men were screened out and homosexual or dissenting men were allowed in, many eventually ordained.

So evident is the tipping of the scales that even *The New York Times* quoted former seminary rector Fr. Donald Cozzens, who said that the Catholic priesthood had become "a gay profession." This has led to the establishment and ad-vancement of a multitude of LGBT-friendly "ministries" whose goal is to so undermine Church teaching that everyone ignores it as they do other teachings on sexual morality.

Homophobic War Cry
Originally aired May 31, 2012

I T'S TIME TO BE AS CLEAR AS A BELL on a current issue. There are people in the Church, many of them in positions of great influence, who are either promoting or allowing the militant homosexual movement. Some of these people are somewhat naïve and may believe what they are doing is for "pastoral" reasons. Others actually disagree—privately or publicly—with the Church's teaching and want to get rid of it in practice, much like was done with contraception. In either case, what is happening is the Church's teaching is being ignored.

Another thing is happening as well. Voices in the Church who point to the authentic teaching are now being labeled homophobic by others *inside the Church.*

First of all, there is no such thing as homophobia. Faithful Catholics aren't "afraid" or "fearful" of men or women with same-sex attraction, like, e.g., people are afraid of spiders or water. That's ridiculous, and it's disingenuous to accuse people of it. Homophobia is a term totally invented by the militant homosexual camp so they could easily label people who believe homosexual acts are immoral as mentally disturbed or even "haters."

There is no such thing as homophobia. No one goes and lies down on a psychiatric couch and seeks help for fear of people with same-sex attraction. Since the term is nothing but a politically charged label, it should never be used in discussions within the Church. But that hasn't stopped various Catholics from throwing the term around and using it against Catholics who are saying nothing more than Church teaching.

There is absolutely no room for that kind of talk inside the Church. The Catholic faith has a vocabulary all its own that does not admit in or compromise with the culture of the day on matters of faith and morals. To accuse someone of being homophobic for something he's written or said, to accuse someone of being homophobic in an effort to silence him by labeling him some kind of social pariah, is totally out of bounds inside the Catholic world. When faithful Catholics talk about the evil of homosexual acts, they do it in reference to the person's eternal destiny. Period.

We receive more than our share of emails and phone calls from people struggling with this heavy cross grateful for the way we express ourselves and demonstrate the truth with charity. But there are others who do not want the Church's teaching spoken of plainly and clearly. They either are homosexual themselves and want the teaching squashed or are friendly toward the cause of militant homosexuality.

Their invective needs to be called out. They claim the label "pastoral" in their approach to this sin, when nothing could be further from the truth. It is never pastoral to allow someone to remain in the dark about their sin and encourage them to remain in it.

Watch out when you hear anyone in the Church tossing around the word "homophobia." It's almost a sure guarantee they have an agenda, or are just plain ignorant.

Weak Men and Homosexuality
Originally aired December 12, 2013

AS YOU LOOK AT POLL AFTER POLL that keeps getting released surveying Catholic opinion on same-sex "marriage," it's impossible not to notice a disturbing trend. First of all, according to each poll, the majority of self-identified Catholics support same-sex marriage. Not surprising, really, when you consider that they overwhelmingly support contraception and, by lesser margins, abortion.

But even more disturbing is the number of young Catholics who support the evil of same-sex marriage, including many among the pro-life crowd. They have simply never been told in any meaningful way that homosexuality is intrinsically disordered and homosexual acts are evil.

Here is the truly ensnaring thing about the whole gay issue. It has been masterfully painted by the diabolical and his agents as being all about "love," and those who oppose it therefore are anti-love—which means hateful and bigoted and all that. Since no one wants to be around mean or bigoted losers, for many young people there is therefore now a built-in cultural road block to the exploration or acceptance of the Faith. It is an absolute masterstroke of the demonic, a two-pronged attack.

The first prong is to destroy or at least severely erode the intellect by dummying down its natural powers of reason, judgment, and discernment and replacing them with their opposites. This has been done largely in the nation's classrooms, but with major assists from the pop culture, where true education has been abandoned, meaning the tried and proven way of taking the intellect through the rigors of memorization and logic and philosophy. What has replaced this is heaping amounts of self-esteem blather and sensitivity chatter.

The second prong of the attack to complete the process of the destruction of the intellect has been a full-out assault to promote the passions and feelings and emotions, centered on a narcissistic concentration of self. The gay rights movement is the perfect example of the triumph of this two-pronged approach: Deaden the intellect; elevate the emotions.

Young people today, a large majority of them, form their opinions about morality not based on the intellect but based on feelings. That is the game-winner for the gay rights movement. And why is it that so many young Catholics have fallen into this trap along with their non-Catholic peers—in fact, even more so? Because too many of the clergy, priests, and bishops are weak men and have not wanted to confront the culture and stand up and say what needs to be said about homosexuality.

In fact, in the particular case of homosexuality, enormous numbers of priests and bishops are actually homosexual themselves, or at the very least overly sympathetic to the sodomite cause. In short, many of them actually have a dog in this fight. They are not just weak men, but weak homosexual men who don't have the spittle and zeal to stand up and say what needs to be said without creating some kind of cognitive dissonance in themselves.

Bishops who capitulate to the culture on sexual and moral issues have become a tradition in the United States for the past fifty years or so. Barely a word was uttered in defense of the Church's teaching on contraception back in the 1960s. In the '70s when abortion arrived on the scene, many of them quickly grew tired and uninterested in preaching about life issues and changed gears to so-called social justice issues.

In the '80s and '90s there was an explosion of divorce and annulments, many of them abuses of the system—and again, weak men under mitres sat back with their mouths shut as Catholic families simply melted down. And then for the past decade, as the homosexual juggernaut has smashed through various cultural institutions, all we've heard is one acquiescence after another. Nary a word from the bishops on the destructive lifestyle of active homosexuals. Nary a word on the general destruction of society in general and humanity at large that comes with the normalization of sodomy.

They are, as a body, simply missing in action on the most important moral issues of the day and then have the gall to transfer importance to other issues that rise to nowhere near the level of these objective evils. They are weak men, exceedingly weak men, who because of their weakness become exceedingly easy tools for Satan to use and manipulate. That Catholic youth would be so uncritically thinking and even totally unaware that they should be thinking about this and other issues, using their spiritual faculty of thought and reason to arrive at truth, is perhaps the single largest indictment against this current crop of leaders.

We hear non-stop about the New Evangelization, yet the very generation that will have to live out this evangelization process has already been poisoned against its most central truths—and it is nearly all owing to today's successors of the Apostles who have walked away from the Faith or its implementation for the sake of their weak psyches that demand the love and adoration and praise of men.

Many of them—too many—are too cowardly to face the firing squad of public opinion by standing up for the truth of Christ. And yet they walk around in a self-delusional cloud babbling "New Evangelization, New Evangelization." Maybe they don't want to face the music on this score, either, but if they think the reinforcements that are coming to take up arms in the culture war are just over the hill, they are twice mistaken.

There aren't any reinforcements, and they aren't just over the hill. The lot of these leaders will be the same as that of the Jewish leaders in Jerusalem, as Titus and his tenth Roman Legion wiped out the city and destroyed the temple.

Satan it seems is pulling out every weapon in his arsenal: Islamic terror in the Middle East, dissent and heterodoxy inside the Church, and a near-violent homosexual movement closing in on the Church from every direction with the aiding and abetting of gay and gay-friendly Churchmen too evil or too blind and weak to respond to the danger.

Pray for the Church and her leaders. Pray in all earnestness.

The Church Is Wrong
Originally aired October 7, 2014

ONCE AGAIN, FROM THE FILES MARKED "What You Will Never Hear in the Catholic Establishment Media," we bring you the case of a couple practicing sodomy from the parish of St. Victoria in Victoria, Minnesota.

First, the background: In September 2014, longtime parish music and liturgy director Jamie Moore civilly and legally married his longtime homosexual partner Garrett at his parents' house, with 160 friends in attendance. So when news got around, someone informed the archdiocese of Minneapolis, Abp. John Nienstedt then had to get involved, Moore and his pastor, Fr. Bob White, met with the archbishop, and Moore ended up resigning.

That's when the fun began: the media reports, the recriminations, the liberal Church of Nice spilling out of the pews, the feminized pastor writing a gushy, emotion-filled, aching letter to the parish. Jamie Moore was also even allowed to write an equally emotion-filled letter to the parish, as if to get in the last word.

The whole affair is sickening on so many levels, it's hard to know where to begin.

How is it the case in the first place that an active homosexual was the music and liturgy director at the parish for nearly eighteen years? Judging from all the media reports and letters in the bulletin, his homosexuality and relationship with Garret was no mystery. Father Bob White even says in his letter to the parish: "The way Jamie came to his decision to marry was consistent with the man I've been proud to call my friend for the last eighteen years. It is an honest and open expression of who he is and how he lives his life."

What else does that mean, other than that he knew Jamie was actively homosexual? It is safe to assume Jamie did not legally marry Garrett after having taken up with him for just a couple of weeks. Every media report says they were longtime partners. So how did Fr. White, "who has been proud to call Jamie his friend for the past eighteen years," not know this?

The point is, he *did* know it and didn't care. In his mind and heart, the Church is wrong. And this is the bigger point: In parish after parish all over the country, all over the West, active homosexuals are given free reign in the schools, liturgy offices, music offices, and so forth—and in not a few cases, the pulpits as well. But it's not just active homosexuals; it's lesbian nuns, couples practicing birth control, uninformed, uneducated religious teachers, and others.

There is no substantial difference between what went on at St. Victoria's parish and what goes on every single Sunday in thousands of parishes all over the place. It's just that this case got a lot of press coverage. In parish after parish after parish, people who do not believe the Catholic faith are in charge. And here's another interesting point to ponder: From the perspective of the Church, why does it matter if two people who have same-sex attraction go and get married civilly? It isn't that they went and got hitched legally that's the problem; it's that they are engaged in a sinful life, living in a state of sin, that's the problem. Such people should not be receiving Holy Communion. They are adding sacrilege to their sin.

Even more, a priest should absolutely not be condoning or giving the slightest appearance of approval to their sin, or to anyone's sin, for that matter. It doesn't matter if it's homosexuality or bank robbery or cohabitation. That is why what this priest did in publishing this letter ratchets this evil up to a whole new level.

In the letter, he writes, "I am happy for Jamie and Garrett and wish them nothing but happiness."

What an evil thing for him to say—a man of God wishing them happiness in a life of evil and wickedness and mortal sin. Is this man spiritually insane? Is he supportive of the homosexual lifestyle because he secretly admires it for himself? He has totally embraced the so-called gay agenda and dressed it up in a soppy letter that could have been written by a lovesick teenage girl, yet the fact that it is from one in a position of authority causes confusion among the faithful—as indeed it is intended to do.

Father White has an entirely different view of the Catholic faith from that of the Catholic Church. He needs to be laicized by the archbishop. It isn't enough simply to accept the resignation of an active homosexual from the parish staff. The man who has secretly, or perhaps not so secretly, supported this evil, this scandal for close to two decades—he is the one who needs to go along with Jamie Moore. Moore at least had the decency to resign.

Father White—who is no father to his people but a spiritual abuser—needs to have the decency to resign as well, not from just the parish, but from the priesthood. He hit the nail on the head in another part of his letter when he wrote: "Perhaps ultimately it's about contrasting visions of what it means to be Church."

That's right. It's *exactly* about contrasting visions of the Church—your wrong, evil, wicked view, and the truth.

It's interesting, if you go through White's letter to the parish, four times the words "emotion" or "feeling" appear. Not once does the word "truth" appear. That's because this is what the Church of Nice is built on: feelings and emotions, not truth. And this is why this half-hearted attempt by the Establishment Church to launch into a New Evangelization will never yield any good fruits, because these philosophical evils are allowed to remain.

And to sidetrack for a moment, according to the likes of Bp. Robert Barron, none of this really matters anyway, because, in his view, we have a reasonable hope that all men are saved: sodomites, sodomy-condoning priests, parishioners who claim the Faith but reject it in its teachings, people who haven't been to confession in ages and don't really believe in personal sin, those who refuse to give intellectual assent to the Faith . . . Not only is Bp. Barron's position ridiculous from a commonsense standpoint, it has no support in Scripture or tradition. It is, in short, not Catholic.

The bishops, in the rare case they do anything at all, do the very least amount possible. It is right that Moore is gone. Now the pastor needs to be removed because he is spiritually abusing his flock. He is not preparing them for life in Heaven, but for an eternity in Hell because he is leading them astray.

This is the Church of Nice in full bloom, a parish rallying around a man in an objective state of evil with the priest leading the charge to support him in his evil because to say anything different would be "mean"—and the bishop in this case doing the least possible thing he can do.

When the cameras and TV crews leave and life returns to normal, these Catholics will be left in their ignorance and sin, supported in that ignorance, willful or otherwise, by the Establishment Church that dare not speak the truth. And of course, the Catholic Establishment media, from blowhard bloggers to more official organs, will keep their silence about the evil, but damn anyone who points to the evil and calls it for what it is.

This is the majority situation in the Church these days. It's beyond "hear no evil, see no evil, speak no evil." It's much more akin to "hear no truth, see no truth, speak no truth"—but with regard to evil, *embrace it*.

This will all come tumbling down soon because God will not be mocked forever. And when it does, God have mercy on us all.

Homofascist Assault
Originally aired February 26, 2015

ANYONE WHO THINKS the homofascist assault is going to end before Catholicism is driven underground in this country is simply out of his mind.

The stand-off in San Francisco was a case that made this point clear. The spectacular archbishop there, Salvatore Cordileone, was duking it out with the homofascist squad and their Democratic political allies, who wanted to conduct probes into archdiocesan Catholic schools under the pretense that some of the teachers may have to be enduring unfair labor restrictions. And what would be so manifestly unfair that the state would have to come in to a Catholic school to protect Catholic school teachers from Catholic doctrine?

And this is the way it's going to go down. Catholics, get ready.

The homofascist crowd is poking and prodding, needling and noodling around looking for a legal opening, some loophole, some pretense to begin silencing Catholic doctrine being taught in Catholic schools. The fact of the matter is they could have just left that to liberal Catholics, who have done a much better job at dismantling the Faith in Catholic schools than social liberals could ever dream of accomplish-ing. But we digress.

The archbishop wanted to clarify and reinforce the morals clauses in employee handbooks, morals based on Church teaching. In short, he wanted Catholic school employees to observe Catholic teaching and not undermine students' edu-cation. But the powerful homofascist machine of the Bay Area went into overdrive, hyperventilating at the slightest sugges-tion that Church teaching should be lived and taught by Catholic teachers while they are teaching students. The horror! If they didn't like it, they should've gone to get another job.

But that common sense doesn't sink into the truly dense, whose intellects are so blinded by their love of sin that they can no longer comprehend truth. This is why this ridiculous approach of Church of Nice adherents of tolerance and dialogue and so on will never succeed. The other side—the homofascists, the enemies of the Church—have no interest in living and let live. They want eradication of anything and everything that pricks their conscience. And it is precisely why men—great men like Salvatore Cordileone and some other good bishops—cannot give in on this sort of thing.

It isn't a point of law that's being fought; that's just the excuse. The real war is the war of conscience. The homofascists and their associated abortion-loving, pornography-using, contraception-enraptured allies need the Church either to no longer exist or to be complicit in their sin by excusing it, rationalizing it, or baptizing it. If leaders in the Church were to ever do that on some grand scale, or even give the impression that they looked like they were doing it, it would relieve the guilt this crowd feels in the depths of their souls.

The Church must always announce the truth of Our Blessed Lord. It is ultimately Satan we are battling, and we must stand up to him. He and his agents on earth, his disciples, his offspring, must have war made on them by the offspring of the Woman—and that is the Church Militant, the Church on earth.

This has nothing to do with "mercy." It's about sex. It's about the Sixth and Ninth Commandments and the Church's refusal to give in on sodomy. And we all know that's what it's about. It's not a point of law or labor practices or workers' rights. It's about sex. And as a little warning: This battle is coming to a town near you, and coming soon. Stand tall.

Gay Knights and Damned Bishops
Originally aired June 2, 2015

IT WOULD SEEM THE TIME HAS COME in the Church to root out one of the most glaring problems that no one in authority seemingly wants to deal with: the whole issue of homo-sexuality, meaning not just the attraction, which is not sinful in itself, but the total capitulation to the militant homosexual agenda by those in the Church.

Capitulation comes in five forms: (1) It can mean being actively gay like many clerics are; (2) it can mean being gay while not practicing yourself, but still being sympathetic to the evil, and so ignoring it when it occurs among fellow clergy; (3) it can mean not being gay yourself at all, but still being sympathetic to friends or family who are, and so ignoring it; (4) it can mean not being gay yourself at all, but not wanting to kill your clerical career, and so you choose to keep your mouth shut and not make gay enemies in the Church; and (5) it can mean not being gay yourself, and not really caring about the issue because you are indifferent and lukewarm and don't really care about much at all.

These are five different, largely unrelated ways you can contribute to the gay malaise of the current crisis in the Church, and it matters little which category a man falls into, because the result for the Body of Christ is the same: devastation for the flock. Take note, deacons, priests, bishops, archbishops, and cardinals: If you are in one of these categories and you die in that state, you will be damned—and you will deserve it.

But the clergy, while being the most responsible because they've received the most grace to be holy because they need it—the clergy are not alone. There are other leaders and voices in the Church who, owing to their stature, are also held to a higher standard. One of those groups is the Knights of Columbus, guilty of constantly flirting with and skirting around this issue of homosexuality within their ranks or support for it, either directly or by negligence.

Take, for example, the recent case of a grand marshal of a local council who was openly gay, civilly married to his homosexual partner, and everyone knew it. He died suddenly, God have mercy on his soul, and the obituary even laid it all out for the whole world to see. His name was David Christopher Peshek. The 51-year-old died of a sudden illness in Walnut Creek, California, just before Christmas in 2014. For most of his life, Peshek was not Catholic. He met his homosexual partner in 2001 in Chicago, moved with him to Providence, Rhode Island in 2004, and then came into the Catholic Church in 2012 under instruction from a priest in the diocese of Providence.

We don't know for certain if the priest knew Peshek was living a life contrary to the Catholic Church as he was catechizing him into it, but if he didn't, it seems incredible. Peshek couldn't have been very quiet about it, because the next year, he and his homosexual partner moved to the Bay Area of California and got civilly married. He joined the parish there of the Cathedral of Christ the Light in Oakland and soon became Grand Knight of the Knights of Columbus Council No. 15919 and a member of the Color Corps and Faithful Scribe of the Knights of Columbus Fourth Degree Francis B. Drass Assembly No. 1880.

Far from remaining hidden, Peshek was about as open as you could be about his civil marriage centered on sodomy. The council knew about it; the parish knew about it—which is why his obituaries are so open and in your face about his lifestyle. So the inevitable question: What has been corrupted in the Knights of Columbus that a local council could feel perfectly at home by not only admitting an open homosexual into their ranks, but a "married" homosexual, and then elect him to the position of leader?

What's wrong with the atmosphere in the Knights of Columbus is the same thing wrong in the Church at large: a loss of faith so great that it isn't even recognized or admitted by those who have lost their faith that they have lost their faith.

Now, we know that not every council is corrupt. There are many fine councils with many dedicated Catholic men in them. And we know that many local councils do fine things for the poor, for the pro-life movement. We even know that national headquarters in Connecticut is oftentimes generous with donations to various goings-on in the Church. These are not at question.

But none of that at bottom matters; those good works have no merit attached to them if these evils are not ad-dressed, if they are ignored, if they are overlooked and dismissed. Let's not forget that it was (in the darkness of the night) two Knights of Columbus lawmakers in New York who cast the deciding votes in favor of same-sex civil marriage there, bowing under intense pressure from Catholic anti-Christ governor Andrew Cuomo. When they did that, there wasn't a word from national headquarters; the reaction from the Knights of Columbus was like a tomb, a ghost town.

Many, many knights have contacted us and said they are fed up with the emphasis on the insurance business and practically nothing on the spiritual. If the case of the openly gay Grand Marshal David Peshek—civilly married, living a public life in a state of opposition to the Church—is any example, these knights have every reason to be fed up.

Once again, this goes on because weak, cowardly, feminine, homosexual, or homosexual-friendly bishops have created the environment where it can go on.

Complicit bishop, are you listening? Do you not realize you are on your way to Hell? When you die, Our Lord and Savior Jesus Christ will pronounce the sentence you have chosen. You will be swarmed by demons, dragged to Satan, and for eternity suffer unspeakable torments. Your hands, anointed at your own ordinations, will burn with an indescribable heat owing to that anointing. And your tortures will be increased because, once you were made bishop, you created new priests. The diabolical will unleash a fury of agony on you the likes of which no one else in the infernal realms will feel. You will be damned shepherds, lost forever, having gone to join the ranks of Judas and all the others before you.

Repent now, publicly, while you still have time. When you die, your corpse will be laid out in your cathedral appearing restful and peaceful. Your soul, however, will never again know anything of peace as you will have Satan as your master and demons as your overlords.

Bad Bishops, Bad Politicos
Originally aired August 11, 2015

SOMETIMES, OFTENTIMES, it takes a good amount of time to see the fruits of our labors come into existence. We plant, we sow, and only in season do we begin to reap what we have sown. This is true with good seed and bad seed. In the 1960s and forward, a lot of bad seed was planted in the Church, mostly by clergy, watered by agenda-driven laity—and now it is all coming to fruit—horrible, rotten, putrid fruit.

Take, for example, the GOP debate in August 2015. In the two separate sessions, seven different Catholics stood on stage fielding various questions. Then came the inevitable—because it is timely—question of same-sex "marriage." Ohio governor and Catholic John Kasich gave the following response: "I'm an old-fashioned guy and I see things old-fashioned. I believe marriage is between one man and one woman."

Okay, first problem: "Old-fashioned"—the term means that morality is based on fashions, time constructs, as emphasized and underscored by his use of the word "old." *Wrong, Governor.* That line of thinking alone would disqualify you from ever getting my vote. You can't reason to truth. I don't care how pro-life you are. One way or the other you will collapse and fail when you are most heavily relied on. The truth of marriage isn't based on time or longevity. It's based on truth—a truth you do not recognize.

Then he admitted he went to the wedding of a friend who happens to be gay: "Just because someone doesn't think like I do doesn't mean I don't love them. I'm going to love them no matter what they do. God loves them unconditionally, and so do I."

The idiocy and complete lack of correspondence to objective truth contained in his statement is appalling. He has no true concept of God or love. It is purely arbitrary. He was raised Catholic, but being in the age range where the betrayal of Catholic clergy was reaching great heights, Kasich drifted away from the truth. That isn't terribly surprising. It happened to tens of millions of Catholics who had no firm grounding in the Faith coupled with a glut of evil, wicked, self-interested clergy who had no concern for their vows, promises, or souls. Kasich has become one of those one in ten Americans who is now an ex-Catholic—34 million of them.

But what of now, the current conditions on the ground? Pay close attention, you Church of Nice dreamers, who imagine things are not as bad as they were "back then," that they have improved miraculously, that truth has been embraced without any repentance or recognition of past sin and requisite need for sorrow. Read what what New York Cardinal Timothy Dolan's golden boy Fr. Jonathan Morris had to say on *Fox and Friends* one Sunday morning when the topic of Kasich's response came up as a discussion point:

> I thought it was brave of him. He knows not everyone is going to like his response. It's a real issue what you have to say—what does my faith tell me to do in some situation? Other people wouldn't have gone to the wedding. He looked at it very seriously and decided this is what his faith told him to do. I congratulate him for it.

Won't someone rid us of this troublesome priest?

What a pathetic response to this ugly situation. A fallen-away Catholic endorsing a sodomite marriage gets congratulations from a Catholic priest for his "bravery." This shouldn't be surprising considering his boss sat on national television himself and declared "Bravo!" for a professed active homosexual, NFL-wannabe Michael Sam.

Father Morris couldn't be more un-Catholic in his response or even less human. First of all, on the mere natural level, how is what Kasich said "brave"? Please, Father, have you been watching the news, reading anything, looking at anything else besides the mirror? Coming out in favor of sex between two men is anything but brave. Practically the whole world supports it, as evidenced by the thunderous applause that broke out among Republican supporters when Kasich said what he said.

When will this effeminate-minded clergy stop painting the picture that supporting anal sex publicly is somehow brave? It isn't. It's evil and misguided. It isn't brave when everyone supports you. It's brave when you go against the crowd for the sake of the truth—what *you* are supposed to be doing, Father.

"He decided this is what his faith told him to do."

Stop. Please, Fr. Morris, just turn in your collar. There is no way in Hades your Catholic faith—the same faith that teaches that this activity is evil and immoral—would tell you to go to such a "wedding," especially when the rationale stated by Kasich was that God loves everyone unconditionally. That is not what is meant by love, God, or unconditional.

Father Morris, sitting on national television, talking to millions, had the perfect opportunity here to teach, to preach truth, to gently, kindly explain why what Kasich said was wrong. But no. In true Church of Nice, "Everyone, look at me being politically correct, never giving offense!" claptrap, he whiffed and chose the popular route instead.

God does love unconditionally. *But he does not save us unconditionally.* "If you love me, you will keep my commandments" (John 14:15).

Our response—the only permissible response to God's unconditional love—is unconditional obedience. Absent that, you go to Hell. This is the only permissible point for a priest of the Catholic Church to make. But for the umpteen-millionth time, yet another Catholic cleric refuses to announce the truth when given the opportunity and places his own soul and the souls of others in eternal jeopardy.

Can we expect a clarification from his boss, Cdl. Timothy Dolan? If you are expecting that from the man who not only led a group of militant gays in the St. Patrick's Day parade but publicly cheered and supported the decision, as they say in New York, *fuhgeddaboutit.*

Men like Cdl. Dolan, Fr. Morris, and countless others have

been badly formed in the Faith—and yes, cardinals and bishops can be badly formed, just like Pope Benedict said they could. Being a priest or bishop is no guarantee of having supernatural faith or making correct moral choices or statements. The collar or mitre is no safeguard against eternal perdition. In fact, in many ways it is a *surer way* to condemnation owing to the great responsibility and authority such a man is given. There is almost no margin for error.

We are seeing a never-ending stream of the bad fruits in the clergy of the past fifty years or so evidenced in the laity. It is without a doubt something for which the clergy will be judged, as Scripture confirms. God help them. But to see these errors in the laity continuing to be upheld and supported and applauded, congratulated even today in the ranks of the clergy, is beyond wicked. It is a sin that consists primarily in supporting the sin instead of correcting it. It is in the end a sin against the Holy Spirit.

Whatever evil was manifest thirty, forty, fifty years ago in those clerics is still going strong today. From Bp. Robert Barron's wicked "No one really goes to Hell" implication to Fr. Morris's support of error in cheering a fallen-away Catholic's misguided immoral decision to attend a gay wedding, the list continues to grow of villainous clergy who will have laid waste attempts to re-energize the Church in Her most critical hour.

These abominations must be challenged, exposed, and confronted.

Spotlight
Originally aired Decemer 3, 2015

PART OF THE WORK OF CREATING a Resistance movement within the Church these days includes defining what precisely needs to be resisted. And this is where it gets ugly. There is much worthy of resistance because, put simply, it's not Catholic; it only looks Catholic. In fact, shining the spotlight on all this so it can be driven out is the precise goal of the Resistance.

It's like locating and then removing a tumor. It's ugly work, but it has to be done. The spotlight has to be shone on all this—which is why the film *Spotlight* is a must-see. It's a well-shot, nicely produced, nicely acted film focusing on the uncovering of the Boston homosexual priest sex abuse scandal, which was the epicenter of the entire scandal back in 2002. It follows along the investigative team from the *Boston Globe* as they learn bit by bit the sinister, sordid activity in which various senior clergy in the archdiocese of Boston were involved.

Make no mistake, that same spirit of evil, so omnipresent in institutional Church establishments, has not gone away. That particular expression of it has gone away for the most part, but the *climate*, the *culture* that allowed this to flourish until the press got their hands on it is still very much alive.

Think about it: An entire establishment, a ruling class, that conspired, threatened, bullied, intimidated, and demeaned children and their parents into silence—where did those men go? We aren't talking about the gay predators. We're talking about the men in collars and mitres, hundreds and hundreds of them all over the country, in seminaries and chanceries and religious houses—the whole network of them. Almost none of them has gone to jail. Not one of the bishops—of which there had to be dozens and dozens—ever went to jail. They weren't even arrested.

Where did all these men go? Where are they today? They are still sitting comfortably inside the fortress of the Establishment Church, that's where. It's an entire network of men who can easily be manipulated by Satan—and indeed they are. How can I say that? How can that charge be made so easily? Because their first love is not for souls but for the protection of the Establishment fortress.

When I was a sophomore at the University of Notre Dame, I met this Establishment up close and personal, and believe me, there isn't a thing "nice" about the Church of Nice. Near the end of my sophomore year, I started receiving anonymous letters through campus mail. At first they were innocent enough. I thought my roommates or other buds were goofing with me. But then they turned dark, laying out sexual fantasies with me at the center of it all. I took all this to a priest on campus who advised me to wait out the storm for the rest of the semester since it was almost over. Nothing more happened—until summer school.

The priest I had gone to for counsel was away on vacation and sent me a letter admitting that he was the author of all the other letters and cards. I was nineteen. He was a priest. I was at Notre Dame, where I had wanted to go my entire life, even trying out to be leprechaun. Notre Dame was my world. The Church environment was my world. And this man, in whom I had confided my fears, turned out to be the very man who was the cause of it all.

On advice, I went to a high-ranking member of the religious community that runs Notre Dame to tell him everything. We met in Hesburgh Library at a desk on the eighth floor. I told him everything. He asked to see the cards and notes and letters. I gave them over to him, and he promised he would take care of everything.

Two weeks later, when I was at my job, mowing fairways on the Notre Dame golf course, campus security came to me and said my presence was required immediately at the Dean of Students office. I was escorted with grass clippings, sweat, and all and brought into a conference room with a big board table, the dean of students on one end and a group of about four or five men in suits and ties huddled together on the other end. They were not introduced to me.

The dean had me sit down on his left, and proceeded to discuss all I had told the priest in the library. The dean, sitting right there in that room, turned the story around on me and accused me of lying. He then brought in the very priest who had written the letters to me. He sat at the dean's right hand—directly across from me. The dean apologized to him for all of this and then asked him to read a testimony.

The priest, wearing his collar and black for the first time I had ever seen, began reading from a prepared statement accusing me of being a wild party guy, out of control, always embellishing stories, firing off accusations that I had a drinking problem and was untrustworthy. While I was no shrinking violet during my college years and did party too often, there wasn't a shred of truth to the larger implications he was making.

I lunged across the table at him, but the size of the table prevented me from actually making contact—and, dare I say, lucky for him. Eventually I had to settle down and restrain myself, but the priest was excused, and again the dean offered an apology to him for all he had been put through. The dean then turned to me and said I had suffered a lot and needed to go to psychological services or I would be kicked out.

It was then that I sprung on them that there was a witness to that confession letter, and the witness was a good friend whose father was the university provost. You could have heard a pin drop. I seized the moment and demanded that he, too, be dragged in off the golf course just as I was—and I wasn't moving from that seat until he was brought in.

Faced with no real choice, they brought him in. They questioned him in my presence. He confirmed everything because he had been with me on lunch break and in my presence when I opened the confession letter. I had handed it to him—in complete shock. He had read the whole thing, likewise in complete shock. He confirmed every bit of this in that board room on that August day in 1981—the day the scales fell from my eyes.

As the dean wrapped up the meeting, he told me they would be in touch with me. I never heard another word about the matter.

These sinister men *hide* behind the Church, hide *in* the Church, executing their plots and schemes to destroy anyone they need to who runs afoul of their ambitions, whether their ambitions are for theological poisoning, or power and money, or sex, or probably a few other agenda items. I wasn't sexually abused, but I was psychologically abused. I lost whatever innocence I had left that day on the second-floor board room of the dean of students.

The Church is bursting at the seams with scoundrels and sinister men like this. They were willing to take a nineteen-year-old kid—who had never dreamed of anything else but going to Notre Dame—and, using the excuse of protecting the name of Notre Dame, expel him.

As I sat through the *Spotlight* film, all these feelings came back to me. As I watched the retelling of all that evil unfold on the screen, as I heard audience members gasp, I was flooded with feelings of shame and rage at the same time—shame for the name of the Church, of Her beauty being hung out to dry by these loathsome, uncaring men, and rage that justice be done.

Today, what do we see in the Church: in some cases the same individual men, or those who were younger when all this was going on and who kept their mouths shut so they could protect a future career as bishop. And these same men and their disciples today allow and promote spiritual abuse by allowing souls to be ruined with their sacrileges and blasphemies and subtle distortions of the Faith with half-baked catechetical programs and their refusal to preach the hard truth and their willingness to commit adultery with the world.

They forsake Christ, His Bride, and His sheep and plow under anyone in their way. They must be stopped. They must be exposed.

As long as men like this hold this kind of power, no one is safe, either with regard to this world or the next, or both. They refuse to be transparent. They take responsibility for nothing. They own up to nothing. They are accountable to no one. They will never respond to any charge except when they answer it with lies and attacks against those blowing the whistle.

Pope Benedict actually expressed gratitude for secular reports exposing the crisis. He added while the press was hostile often in its reporting, the Church could not have been attacked as She had "had it not been for the evil in the Church."

Had it not been for the evil in the Church. That evil, motivated by something other than a love for souls, has not gone away. It has simply shifted strategies. The great evil—and it was *great*—inflicted on the bodies and psyches of so many innocent is eclipsed only by the greater evil inflicted on the souls of so many more. The spotlight needs to keep shining.

Half of Priests and Bishops Are Gay
Originally aired January 11, 2016

HERE'S THE HEADLINE: As many as half of priests and bishops in the United States may be homosexual.

Back in 2000, just as news of the homosexual priest sex abuse crisis was beginning to break, the *Kansas City Star* did an in-depth exposé on a horrible topic: the large number of homosexual priests dying of AIDS. The newspaper's reporting brought to public light, for the first time on this kind of scale, the issue of homosexuality in the priesthood—albeit through the tragic lens of AIDS.

The newspaper conducted extensive research into the related issues of AIDS and homosexuality within clerical ranks and religious communities. Far from denying the paper's stories, the bishop of Kansas City at the time, Raymond Boland, admitted the findings were true and said, "Much as we would regret it, it shows that human nature is human nature."

The issue of the AIDS deaths aside (God rest their souls), it reveals the reality of homosexuality in the ranks of the ordained—and not just its presence, but its *overwhelming* presence.

The same time the *Kansas City Star* was publishing its series of reports, another report, much less known, was also being circulated, this time in private meetings in the Church. It was prepared by the National Federation of Priests' Councils, a group born from the liberal days of the Sexual Revolution in the wake of Vatican II.

In its thirty-four pages is a vivid discussion of the AIDS crisis at the time among priests owing to the large number of homosexual men in the presbyterate. Its contents contain discussions of how each diocese and religious order should go about preparing for the financial strain of caring for so many priests with AIDS. It makes recommendations about whether to screen seminarians for HIV, a policy eventually adopted across the country. Experts in the field talk about the arrested psychosexual development of homosexual men in the seminary and the priesthood.

The research and investigations being conducted back in 2000, both from the clerical organization and secular media outlets, began unearthing disturbing parallels. Priests and even bishops were dying from AIDS at an alarming rate. In 1995, New York auxiliary bishop Emerson Moore died of AIDS in a Minnesota hospice. Across the country, estimates from assorted experts put the number of Catholic priests dying from the disease at as high as 1,000 in roughly a ten to fifteen year span. Numbers were showing that priests were becoming infected and dying at a rate of as high as ten times the national average.

All this strongly suggested that the number of homosexual men in the Catholic priesthood was much higher than even the most suspicious had guessed. It wasn't long before the truth started coming out, tied as it was to the AIDS death news.

Numerous independent sources inside the Church began polling and interviewing and questioning and researching. Their results were jaw-dropping. One survey done by a New Jersey Franciscan priest and researcher revealed that 45 percent of 500 priests surveyed volunteered that they were gay and that one in four of them had AIDS, proving rampant promiscuity.

Over the years, a large number of surveys, polls, and research have produced a wide range of estimates of the percentage of men in the ranks of the ordained who are homosexual: as low as fifteen percent all the way up to fifty-eight percent. That compares to the overall national percentage of about one and a half percent.

Even if the lowball estimate of fifteen percent is right, it would still be ten times the national average. And if the high end is closer to reality, then more than half of all men in the priesthood and episcopate are homosexual, and would represent a population almost fifty times the national average.

Where are we going with all this? It underscores some of our reports that the Church in America and other countries in the West is controlled by a homosexual collective, the most in-your-face example of which is the outlandish scandal and cover-up in the archdiocese of New York involving Fr. Peter Miqueli and his gay-for-pay boyfriend Keith Crist, who acted with the knowledge and protection not only of the vicar general, Msgr. Greg Mustaciuolo, but also, sources say, of Cdl. Edwin O'Brien.

The destruction rained down on innocent souls in the care of Cdl. Timothy Dolan and his New York archdiocese chancery is shameful, scandalous, sinful—and it has happened as a result of one accused homosexual priest and the extensive cover-up and excusing of his actions by influential and high-ranking officials in the chancery and even in Rome.

In a nutshell: The American Catholic Church is largely con-trolled by homosexual clergy and their allies. Those not in the network are powerless to confront it owing to its vast influence and fear factor, as well as a failure to understand how it operates. The Catholic Establishment media won't get within a million miles of this issue because they too are afraid.

But lay faithful and independent Catholic media outlets like Church Militant as well as others don't suffer from being wedded to the Establishment. It's why we can pour resources into a story like the New York scandal and use it as a spring-board to help Catholics understand the larger stakes involved. The power of this homosexual collective must be broken, and the first step in that is exposing it.

Over the past half century, tens of thousands of homosexual men have been recruited and admitted into the priesthood. Many of them went on to be serial abusers. But others, large numbers of them, have used the Church as a means to deal with their own pyschosexual drama and laid waste to the faith of tens of millions in the process.

This evil must be dragged into the light and those responsible dealt with.

Not Born That Way
Originally aired April 27, 2016

B ACK IN THE 1990s, the Human Genome Project was in
all the headlines. Scientists were at last able to unravel
the DNA structure of humans and look at every single
microscopic truth of our existence. Much buzz surrounded
the issue of the so-called "gay gene," that missing piece in the
gay lobby's much-vaunted public relations machine that
would at last prove that homosexuality was hardwired into
some human beings—that they were, in short, "born that
way."

The problem is that no such gene was ever discovered,
because no such gene exists, because no one actually is born
that way.

The cultural belief that homosexuality is just an equal yet
alternative sexuality is a lie. It is an alternative but broken
sexuality. There is only one sexuality; nature has ordained
that. But there are various ways in which that single sexuality
can be broken, twisted, and misapplied. So-called homosexuality is just one of those ways.

In the case of all these manifestations of a broken, damaged,
not properly ordered sexuality, something went wrong in the
past. And quite often, what went wrong goes back to beyond
the person's memory, things that happened or didn't happen
at such a young age that the afflicted person truthfully has no
conscious memory of anything. So to them, it does appear in
their conscious minds that they were born that way because
as far back as they can remember, this is how they were.

But that's the very point: as far back as they can remember—
the problem being they can't remember back far enough.
They have no memory of any other self-perception. How
many of us have any substantive recall (in anything we would
now consider significant) of our lives before five years old?
Certainly, we have some fleeting memory of various events
here and there, but no real recall of life on a day-to-day basis

like we do as adults. Those first few years are hugely important in the development of a child; they set the foundation,
and as the saying goes, as the sapling is bent, so grows the
tree.

Somewhere, way back then, psychologists point to that as a
major period in our psychosexual formation—how we relate
to Dad, Mom, others. All kinds of messages, stimuli, etc., are
being received into our tiny little minds and being processed,
and that processing forms our self-understanding.

We are, of course, unaware of all this going on, just as we are
unaware that our bodies are undergoing massive changes preparing us for adolescence and adulthood. At one point we are
"done," meaning we emerge into the world of daily
consciousness, with memory and self-perception and all that
which makes us able to function in day-to-day life. But what
happened way back then, what processed in the quiet, unseen
world of our minds, is absolutely important and foundational
and carries forward.

Does anyone really think or want to suggest that early childhood doesn't really count for very much? To discount all that
and simply say "I was born that way" is a massively ignorant
and uninformed statement and conclusion. But it is helpful in
creating an excuse not to deal with the pain of dismantling all
that was improperly formed. No one wants to do that; it's
difficult, painful, humbling work.

No one wants to admit that his entire self-perception around
which he's built and fashioned his life, thoughts, opinions,
worldview, etc. has been one big lie. But that doesn't alter the
objective fact that it is a lie. Conceiving of oneself in terms of
being a homosexual isn't the only damage that can emerge
from a pained childhood. Pain and its avoidance can manifest
in all kinds of ways. But this particular manifestation is
proving to be extremely injurious to individuals in and out of
the Church, including among clergy and laity.

It would even be easy to make the argument that on the list of
things afflicting the Church and blunting Her mission today,

among the top three would be this issue of a broken sexuality, manifesting under a self-perception of homosexuality. And this doesn't necessarily even have to be an active homosexuality.

An ordained man of God who in the quiet of his mind, whether he accepts it or not, detects in himself a strain of homosexuality can be injurious to souls. This is why the acceptance or accommodation of this sexuality or the lack of willingness to confront it among Church leaders is so dangerous to the faithful. The message is not being sufficiently preached that *no one is created by God as a homosexual.*

The reasons it's not being preached are varied, of course, including fear of reprisal from militant homosexuals, or the psychological inability among some to deal with the issue in themselves, or fear of losing money from a poorly catechized laity. Whatever the reason, sermons need to be preached that you are *not* born that way, but can be re-*born this* way, the way of the Catholic Church in Her sacraments and faithful adherence to Her sacred teachings.

God wills that all men come to the truth and be saved. There is a block to the truth when a person is living a lie and living that lie because he's afraid of resurfacing pain for which he is not responsible.

There is no pain in the world that Almighty God cannot pull you from. "I have said this to you, that in me you may have peace. In the world you have tribulation; but be of good cheer, I have overcome the world" (John 16:33).

Chapter Eight

Masculinity

A N EARLY TWENTIETH-CENTURY AUTHOR once wrote, "Feminism has liberated women from the natural dignity of their sex and turned them into inferior men." What the author might have added to complete the thought is that radical feminism has also turned *men* into inferior men.

One of the problems in the Church today—better stated, one of the fuels powering the problems in the Church today—is the assault against the masculine in the cause of the feminine. Virtually all vestiges of masculinity have been erased in the Church. The priesthood has become associated with the effeminate; religious activity in general is associated with the feminine; all spiritual strength seems to have been sapped from the life of the Church. Objective dogma and doctrine have been downplayed while emotions-based experiences are emphasized.

The virtues are no longer seen as ways to live in a masculine manner. The root word of virtue, *vir*, is Latin for "man." The heart of the masculine is to sacrifice for the sake of the feminine, to die if necessary for the community, epitomized by the feminine. For centuries this was shot through the culture and was exhibited in a hundred different ways a day. Even simple things like holding the door open for a lady was a small reflection of this. Today you'd be labeled a misogynistic pig for doing so, and maybe have your career threatened; you might even be sued.

When this mindset gets into the Church (which it very much has), the relationship between God and man, between Christ and His Bride, the Church starts to be misunderstood, with all the attendant dangerous consequences. The Mass, for example, loses its divinely mandated character of a sacrifice, and is lowered to the level of a friendly community meal where the focus is on fellowship and emotions.

The loss of masculine identity has wounded the Church in the West so deeply that it's difficult to imagine its survival under the current hegemony of feminism.

Sex and Morality
Originally aired March 19, 2012

PERHAPS THE PRIMARY MEANS by which Satan attacks the concept of authentic masculinity is by distorting men's understanding of sexuality. Society teaches men that sex is for pleasure, that it's fine to have sex outside of the sacred bond of marriage to one woman, and that the primary function of sex is not for the conceiving and rearing of children in order to make them saints and future citizens of Heaven, but rather for self-gratification. This twisted understanding of masculinity has resulted in a widespread hook-up culture on college campuses, one-night stands, cohabitation, adultery, homosexual relationships.

To be sure, the problem isn't relegated only to men, but because this is the primary means by which Satan attacks the masculine, it must be addressed, particularly for those men sincerely striving to follow Church teaching but who struggle with the continual onslaught of sexually suggestive imagery all over the media, whether it's on TV, the internet, magazines, or highway billboards. The sad fact is that leaders in the Church hardly ever address sexual morality from the pulpit, so boys and men aren't getting the guidance they need. And parents are often reluctant to approach this subject with their teenage children because they feel awkward or embarrassed.

The topic here is masturbation. And because it is a sin of the sexual dimension, it has the possibility of inflicting great harm or damage on the soul. It can easily lead to habit and open the door to other gravely disordered actions, like pornography, which can then lead to other, even worse sins.

The Church teaches that masturbation is grievously wrong, a gravely disordered act. Why? First, it demonstrates a loss of respect for the sanctity of the sexual gift. Sex, by its very nature, is meant to be an act of intimacy between two persons, a mutual exchange of full giving and love, a physical demonstration of the complementarity between the sexes.

Masturbation ignores all this. It turns the person inward on himself and produces a fantasy life in the mind of the person that can serve to detach him increasingly from reality, producing fertile ground to become a victim to pornography as well as keeping sexual thoughts ever active in the mind. It's not surprising that many people, especially the young, fall into the habit of masturbation, a kind of addiction. They begin to order the affairs of their life around such times. And because this particular act carries with it such intense physical pleasure, it can easily develop into a place of psychological retreat for the lonely, the angry, or the isolated.

The psychological impact can result in the exact opposite of what such people need, which is to emerge from their inner selves and form meaningful, healthy relationships with others and view themselves in the light of reality and not in the light of sexual fantasy. There can be little doubt that, given the temptations so numerous in the world today, this particular sin should be viewed as the beginning of the collapse of Catholic morality.

Masturbation is virtually celebrated in the entertainment media as something only slightly embarrassing and mostly humorous. This aids in downplaying it as a sin. Many young Catholics today aren't even aware that masturbation is a sin, and a serious one at that. In the sacrament of confession, the gravity of this sin, as well as sin in general, is greatly downplayed. We see the same approach to sin in the academic world, where any notion of sin and its gravity is nearly totally destroyed.

But for young Catholics, this particular sin is usually the first difficult challenge to their personal morality. To fail to conquer this area of their lives can easily set the stage for even greater moral failings farther down the road. There is, of course, the response of the popular culture that masturbation is normal, that everyone does it, so what's the big deal? But many things can be considered normal and still be wrong.

The Church often understands the word "normal" in the context of "usual" or "common" for human beings weakened by the material effects of original sin. It is, for example, normal for people to get sick, lose their tempers, lie, cheat, gossip—yet none of these should be thought of as good. For some people arriving late to work or leaving early is quite normal, but ask their boss or colleagues if such "normal" behavior is good, and you will undoubtedly receive an unambiguous response—in the negative.

We are all called to be on the path to holiness. Such a journey involves many struggles and desires that must be mastered. This is one such struggle.

A Sexual Fantasy World
Originally aired March 20, 2012

THE TOPIC OF MASTURBATION is rarely discussed openly because of its deep personal nature and possible embarrassment to those discussing it. But it is a serious topic. Because a large number of Church Militant's audience is male, it shouldn't be a surprise that we receive a not insignificant number of emails or in-person communications about this topic. It almost always comes up in one form or another whenever there is a group of young people around.

The simple truth about this teaching is that it has not been stated clearly from the pulpit or in the confessional. The number of young people who have said to us that some priests routinely dismiss the gravity of this sin, some going so far as to say that it isn't a sin at all, has been a bit of an eye-opener. Those priests are wrong. Masturbation is a grave misuse, or even more plainly, *abuse*, of our sexual powers.

We talked about some of the spiritual aspects of this in the previous segment, and will come back to that discussion later. For now, it might be helpful to discuss the psychological aspects of this act, especially if it becomes habit-forming.

A grave consequence of masturbation is that it turns the person's thoughts in on himself by creating a fantasy world, a retreat into a private arena of sexual power where everything revolves around personal bodily pleasure and any other people that are present in the mind are figments of the imagination, or imagined versions of real people. Continued, repeated retreat into this world can obscure the thoughts of a young man or woman when they are in the real world. They can easily begin to transfer their fantasies on to actual people and lose touch with reality.

They begin to see them, at least in part, as something different from and less than what they are—as objects to be used for self-gratification. That is very wrong, and a great injury to the dignity of the person being objectified. Moreover, because of the pleasure associated with sexual release, this becomes a reinforcing behavior and habit. And it has the added dimension of becoming a place where a young and developing mind can go to escape the inevitable pain and hurt associated with growing up.

The habit of masturbation has all the earmarks of becoming a trap, psychological as well as physical. It can quickly become a place to hide from pain and emotional hurt, to create a world where fantasy replaces reality, all reinforced by intense physical pleasure. Not only is this a dangerous situation for anybody, it poses an especially difficult challenge for Catholics, or for any Christians, for that matter. The road through life for a follower of Our Blessed Lord is one strewn with suffering—and not just suffering for its own sake, but for the sake of the other.

Suffering and pain serve a purifying role for the follower of Christ, so they are not aspects of reality from which to run but rather to be embraced and incorporated into one's life. This isn't to say one should go in search of suffering, but rather to accept it and use it constructively when it does come. But this is nearly impossible for the young soul trapped in a habit of masturbation. On the contrary, pain and suffering are viewed as something to be avoided at all costs, even to the creation of an alternate reality.

How many young people have developed this habit and are thereby stunting their spiritual and psychological growth? The privacy often demanded and desired by the young can frequently involve this issue. For effective maturation, an openness to the world, a willingness to engage with it, is necessary. Any type of self-created, alternate reality runs contrary to this whole schema. Even when a person is engaging with reality, if he's transferring aspects of a fantasy onto reality, his engagement is an immature one. This poses a real danger to a young person as he moves into adulthood.

Pain, and a fantasy-driven desire to escape from it, becomes too consuming for him to advance in such a way that he can establish healthy interpersonal relationships and view reality in a realistic way. People he sees in the real world become objects he manipulates in his fantasies. Add to all of this the fact that as long as nothing stops this behavior, he never stands up like a man and confronts the pain in his life. He never learns to fight, but only to retreat. Sin not only has consequences in the next life, but in this life as well.

Battling Sexual Sin
Originally aired March 21, 2012

W E SHOULD FIRST DISTINGUISH between the young and the not-so-young confronting the sin of masturbation in their lives. Those who have developed a long-standing habit of sin in this area face a somewhat different set of struggles from those who are just falling into the habit.

For those who are younger—teenagers, young adults—it can be discouraging to try and avoid the habit. Physical changes to the body's hormonal system as well as the psychological maturation process can lead to a feeling of near-compulsion. The entertainment world to which most young people are exposed makes light of masturbation and sexual temptation in the form of images, conversations, and music and are served up as part of a daily diet; it may seem impossible not to give in to this particular sin.

For those young people who understand the gravity of this sin and are making a serious effort to overcome it, it can become discouraging and draining and even create a "throw in the towel" attitude. It's easy to succumb to all those voices around you saying things like "It's ok, everybody's doing it. No big deal." What we need to recognize in those types of temptations is that they aren't so much temptations of the flesh as they are temptations to distort your intellect. They obviously have reference to the flesh, to a physical sexual act, but they are presented to your intellect, not to your flesh.

Rationalizations necessarily appeal to our rational natures, our thought process. This is why it is so important, so very important, to make sure that your mind, your intellect, is a bastion of truth and logic. God gave you a mind to be able to reason to truth, and when a temptation comes along that assails your intellect, you must be equipped to fight back intellectually.

This is, after all, how the serpent got to Eve; he snaked around the tree and spoke with her, proposing things for her intellect. She makes this abundantly clear when she responds to God that the serpent "beguiled me, and I ate" (Genesis 3:13). The temptation to sexual sin, especially masturbation, is actually an opportunity to grow. All temptation is. Temptation is the chance to choose the good, to do the right.

While we don't like them when they show up, we need to consider that there is a silver lining. We also have to ask why we don't like temptation. The bottom-line answer is always the same: because down deep we know we are weak and are fearful that we'll fall. We know our own history. And yes, left to our human natures, we often fall and give in. It's our nature to be inclined toward sin. In the depths of our fallen natures, it appeals to us, we enjoy it, we sacrifice our intellects, dull as they are, and we give in.

What prevents us from giving in, the only thing that really can, is *grace*. The life of God is what transforms the life of our fallen nature. We must desire to overcome sin, we must want to be a Champion, which means we must be willing to sacrifice, to pay the price. It is in the struggle that the man is forged. In order to engage in the struggle, we must understand, comprehend, intellectualize everything that is being laid out before us. It takes a tremendous act of the will to conquer sin, a hero's will, in fact.

Allowing oneself to become discouraged is for cowards. It's the very meaning of the word "dis-couraged"—"without courage." Young men aren't called to be cowards; they are called to great heights of power and glory, to stand in the glory of God and use their powers for the good of others. Getting discouraged is exactly what your enemy wants. Discouragement further weakens you, it softens you up and makes you much more vulnerable when the next assault comes. And a horrible cycle begins.

Behind that cycle is a self-view that is truly sad, a man reduced to a weak boy. But don't be discouraged. Don't see yourself as unable to overcome sin. Since this involves a sin, it will take grace to overcome it. And the good news is what the good news has always been, and that is that *grace abounds*.

Conquering Sexual Sin
Originally aired March 22, 2012

WHEN WE DISCUSS MASTURBATION, it's important to help people understand that, like all sin, it can be conquered. There is much reason for hope. For the faithful Catholic, in fact, there must develop a certitude that sin can be vanquished, and not just masturbation, but all sin. It is the *raison d'être* for being Catholic.

As we have discussed, masturbation has difficult hurdles built in that makes first struggling with and then conquering this sin more difficult perhaps than other sins. Because it is a sin of the flesh, it has an especially strong draw and can easily become habitual. But just because it is often more difficult to battle and overcome than many other sins doesn't mean that one is excused from the battle. In fact, it's just the opposite. It is precisely because it is for many people so difficult that it must be fought against strongly and with much more intensity.

Some practical steps include spending time in reflection, considering the circumstances of when the greatest times of temptations manifest themselves. For example, is it late at night lying in bed before sleep? How about waking hours? If one or both of those times are when the occasion of sin easily presents itself, then one practical suggestion is simply to get out of bed. If the bed is the greatest occasion of sin, then get up and do something else. Don't just lie there.

It is a good idea, highly recommended, in fact, to get some holy water and sprinkle some on your sheets immediately before getting into bed while calling on your angels to protect you from the temptation or give you the strength to overcome it. If you do not have some kind of sacramental in plain view in your bedroom, get one—a crucifix, a statue, a painting. Since temptation is suggested almost always first to the imagination, strive to put something else in your imagination and force the evil thoughts out.

It is a fact that the human mind can only contain one thought at a time. While many can and oftentimes do race through in quick succession, the mind cannot hold more than one thought at any single moment. Use that fact as a weapon in your favor. It might also be a good idea to have a crucifix on your bed or your night stand. When temptation comes, grab that crucifix and concentrate on it intensely.

If you are out and about and various scenes or people come into your presence that you know are likely to come back to your imagination later in times of temptation, look away from them as quickly as you can, calling on your angel or Our Blessed Mother to come to you immediately. Demons cannot long abide in the presence of the power of the angels and the radiance of the Blessed Mother. All you have to do is ask.

And as a little aside, do not become discouraged that you are subject to temptation, even if it is a hundred times a day. Remember that even Our Blessed Lord Himself, because He permitted it, allowed Himself to undergo temptation in His humanity. He knows your struggle.

And here is a warning: If you have been trapped in this sin and it has become habit, rest assured that when you begin to try and wrest yourself free from it, the diabolical will notice and come at you more strongly, like a wretched master brutalizing a slave trying to break free. Frankly, in your will, tell them to go to Hell where they belong. You are a son of God and you have been created to stand up as freemen. Hell has no claim on you at all; you belong to God. The only power Hell has over you is that which you give it.

Alongside the increase you will most likely feel in temptation, you will also be aware of the increase in grace poured out on you. If you've been baptized and confirmed, all you have to do is to, so to speak, activate the power of the Holy Spirit in you. You are not slaves to Hell but sons of the Most High, and He is calling you to *fight*, to call on Him to come to your assistance. All the saints and angels, the whole heavenly court, are on your side. Never forget that.

Fill your mind with knowledge of them. Throw out the funk of sexual filth and replace it with the beauty of Heaven. You do this by reading about the saints, watching or listening to DVDs or podcasts about the glories of the Faith. Another benefit of this life that we oftentimes don't recognize as a benefit is this simple reality: There are only twenty-four hours in a day. For some of those hours we are unconscious, leaving a limited number of hours in which to have to do battle. If we spend our free time in pursuit of pure, noble, faith-filled thoughts, there is that much less time for the demonic to get inside our heads. He eventually runs out of time.

Try to find a wise and holy spiritual director, one you can be totally open with about whatever struggles you have in this area. Avail yourself of the sacrament of confession regularly, meaning at the bare minimum every two weeks, perhaps with rare exception because of travel or bad timing three weeks, but never anything less. Go to adoration and just be with Jesus. Even if you don't have a regularly scheduled time each week, do little drop-ins even for a few minutes. He is your final end, after all.

Pray the daily Rosary, and engage in frequent conversation, little chats, even jokes, with your guardian angel. These beings love you with an intensity of love we cannot imagine this side of death, so don't neglect your angel. Talk with him. He was chosen by God specifically for you, to help you on the way to Heaven. He is your friend throughout life, so don't neglect him. Call on him for help whenever you face temptation.

Keep the spiritual at the top of your mind, and the devil will eventually flee. "Resist the devil and he will flee from you" (James 4:7). He will be beaten back and you will have Heaven to thank, and Heaven will guard you and be your sure defense.

As Psalm 144:1–2 says:

> "Blessed be the Lord, my rock,
> who trains my hands for war,

and my fingers for battle;
my rock and my fortress,
　　my stronghold and my deliverer,
my shield and he in whom I take refuge,
　　who subdues the peoples under him."

Fight, my brothers, fight. Don't be discouraged. Do not count the lost battles but revel in the victories, even if they might be few early on. What's important is to fight. The soul who gains Heaven is the one who dies fighting.

The Sexual Gateway Sin
Originally aired March 23, 2012

I N MANY WAYS, masturbation is a type of gateway drug—a sin that can quickly and easily become habitual and open the floodgates for many other sexual sins. Since the mind is so powerful, once it is formed and confirmed in the habit of sin, it is extremely difficult to break the habit because it has become so engrained. When the mind becomes habitually fixated, it is regularly open to that which stimulates it.

This is true in the virtues as well as the vices. What else are virtues or vices other than habits that are either good or bad? Develop good habits and you will tend to be virtuous. Develop bad habits and you will tend to be vice-filled. There's nothing hard to grasp there. Without a doubt, a mind filled with sexual thoughts will begin to look for opportunities to encourage even more sexual thoughts. For such is the nature of the sexual appetite; it is never satiated. It must be channeled correctly and conquered, not compromised with.

With the abundance of pornography on the internet, which provides anonymity, the soul trapped in the habit of masturbation faces nearly insurmountable odds that he will become engulfed in internet porn. And when those floodgates are opened, when there is virtually nothing in one's daily life to hold back the poison, a person can become enslaved before he even knows what hit him. Masturbation and pornography, especially internet porn, are intrinsically linked. One feeds the other, and that is, in fact, the goal of purveyors of internet porn—to get a soul trapped by having the man become addicted while making a small fortune off him in the process. This habit must be avoided at all costs, and if you find yourself in it and unable to walk away, you must seek help and counsel outside yourself to hold you accountable on the road to quitting.

There are also larger concerns in this spiritual war other than just the habit. There is the fallout from the habit. For example, if you have fallen in this particular area, you should forgo reception of Holy Communion. The *Catechism of the*

Catholic Church makes clear that this is intrinsically evil. Now, if you are a young man and attend Mass with family or friends and are afraid that a direct question may be posed to you about why you did not receive, you can always eat something before Mass and truthfully answer that you broke the fast. You have a right to your good name and need not disclose your sin to the world. Nonetheless, you need to get to confession as soon as you can. Part of the plan to overcome bad habits is to practice good ones, and there are no better habits to practice than faithful reception of the sacraments.

And speaking of the sacraments, it is unfortunately the case for a variety of reasons that many priests in the confessional downplay the gravity of this sin. If they do, they are failing their sheep, the souls entrusted to their care. They sometimes say all someone has to do is make an act of contrition and then they can go to Holy Communion. No. The sin needs absolution. The man needs to be accountable and experience the consequences of his actions.

Although it's a delicate area to discuss, we have heard intimacies from priests themselves who have struggled with this sin. They also need to go to confession right away, and if at all possible, not to offer the Holy Sacrifice of the Mass in this condition. The Sacrifice of the Mass is, of course, not made invalid by the state of the soul of the priest. But for the good of the priest's soul, this sin must be attended to as quickly as possible.

We all need to pray for our priests because of the high demands on them and the constant temptation they face from Satan, who holds them in particular contempt. This could become a trap for them as well. And unlike the laity, they might not have access to frequent confession because of geographical distances or an acute shortage of priests in their area. It's also a sad fact that like hundreds of millions of the laity, many priests were given bad counsel in this area, and if they are teaching error, they too might be rationalizing this sin, thereby limiting their interior priestly lives.

We are all subject to concupiscence, and often this sin is an outward expression of something much deeper—anger or loneliness or something else—and it requires patience but firmness as well. Ultimately, we must seek to vanquish it, as we seek to vanquish all evil from our lives out of love for Our Blessed Lord. Many people have told us about their own lifelong struggle with this sin and others of their victory after a long and difficult slog. One fellow even shared with us that now freed from this through prayer and the sacraments, he is enrolling in seminary in the fall.

God is greater than any sin or addiction to sin. Overcoming sin involves in many instances taking stock—personal, spiritual, psychological inventory—and making an honest and truthful assessment of where we stand before God in our deepest conscience. It is Satan, your enemy, who wants you to live in the shame or accept that it is no big deal so you remain in the sin.

With regard to overcoming sin in the battle to fight off your adversary, the ancient serpent, especially in the area of sexual sin, perhaps the best words Our Blessed Lord ever spoke is the simple phrase, "If you continue in my word, you are truly my disciples, and you will know the truth, and the truth will make you free" (John 8:31–32).

The Democrats' War on Men
Originally aired September 5, 2012

THERE IS SO MUCH IN COMMON between the old and dying modernist guard in the Church and the Democratic Party that it's sometimes frightening. Take, for example, the Democrats' charge that Republicans are waging a "war on women." The real truth is that Democrats have been waging a war on men for decades—or perhaps more accurately, a war on the masculine.

The Women's Lib movement of the 1960s through 1990s found a natural home among the immoral miscreants who seized control of the Democratic Party at about the same time. Radical feminism dressed itself up as the noble goal of "equality," but what it really sought was sameness, as in no distinction between the genders. So now, decades later, what we have is a female population not only as crude and sexually exploitive as their male counterparts, with no idea of modesty, but a male population denuded of practically every aspect of manliness.

From modern male film actors and models who look more like women than men, to a celebration of active, proud homosexuals who strut around deliberately displaying more swish than any woman pounding her way down a fashion catwalk, even the outward appearance of the masculine has been sucked out of the culture.

But the rot is far deeper than what you see on the surface. Beneath the upper-level destruction of masculine imagery there has been a far deeper destruction of manliness. Males have been encouraged to abandon their unique roles as fathers, protectors, and guardians of the community and give in to their passions, which results in using and abusing women and encouraging the murder of their children when the contraception fails.

All that is bad about the masculine—anger, pride, self-centeredness, laziness, lack of desire, lack of discipline, lack of self-control, lack of initiative to protect and sacrifice—has been elevated and encouraged by the Democratic Party in policy after policy. From abortion to homosexuality to no-fault divorce to fornication—you name it, and the Democratic Party is right there with a new law in hand ready to make it all come true.

Case in point: The icon of Democrats, in some ways the man called on to, ironically enough, preserve Obama's miserable presidency was Bill Clinton. Could there possibly be a larger, more loathsome example of masculinity striding on to stage amid throngs of wild cheering? This man deserves contempt, yet he is the leading example of what manhood has become: a philandering, adulterous, fornicating, spiteful liar who had his law license yanked and was impeached for perjury; an abuser of young interns (remember Monica Lewinsky?); a wife-cheater so notorious that his Arkansas cronies couldn't keep up with his sexual escapades and had to employ what Hillary was credited with calling "the bimbo squad"—this man is the hero of the Democrats.

But just as the Democrats have encouraged the trouncing of the masculine in the culture at large, so too have weak men in the Church allowed those same forces to establish more than a foothold inside thousands of parishes and other Catholic centers. From massively effeminate clergy, encouraged to join the ranks, to loud-mouthed, liberal nuns whose only prayer seems to be that they be changed into men, to the Church of Nice crowd encouraging an atmosphere so feminized in the Church (and yes, that includes altar girls) that young men want nothing to do with it, the rapidly disappearing masculine element of the Church has taken its toll.

Men who are Catholic don't drop out of the sky. They grow up in the same highly feminized culture as everyone else. They see the same advertisements, go to the same movies, hear the same music, and have the same feminized male role models shoved on them as everyone else in the culture does. If there is anywhere they should be able to go and escape the girly-man bombardment, it should be the Church—the most masculine of institutions ever formed because it was formed by the perfect Man Himself: Jesus Christ.

Yet the priesthood, where the masculine is (or should be) most visibly present, has been overrun by the radical feminine: priests and bishops afraid to call a spade a spade because someone's feelings might be hurt or someone might be offended; bishops who encourage an off-the-wall theology never before seen in 2,000 years of sacred history, where the emphasis is taken off God the *Father* and placed on the community of hand-holding, meal-sharing sissies; clergy who run after and seek the approval of every person they can because, like love-sick high school girls, they need to have their feelings affirmed. So they spend their clerical lives always looking for compromise and consensus instead of being men and doing what men do, which is to make a decision in truth and stick to it.

They pander non-stop to these feminized forces and rule by emotion and fear rather than by logic, and in the process they have become active participants in the destruction of the body of Christ.

Both the feminine and the masculine have great strengths and great weaknesses. And when the bad side of each rules the day, in both the Church and the culture, mankind is in for one hell of struggle. What has happened in both the culture and the Church has been a war on the masculine, and all you have to do is look around and see the destruction, especially in the Church, to figure out who's winning.

Satan and Women's Liberation
Originally aired March 24, 2014

M AN CAN NEVER HOPE to outsmart a demon, especially the Demon. Case in point: the Women's Liberation Movement of the 1960s, which has had a profound effect on the current chaos reigning in the culture. It was marketed, if you will, as a means to free women, to liberate them from the oppression of the tyrannical male rule—hence "women's liberation," or women's lib.

But while the fingerprints of the diabolical are all over that movement, what is less obvious is the real goal of the demonic—not so much the alleged "freeing of women" but the diminishing of men. The immediate effect has been the masculinizing of women, but the intended effect by the demonic has always been the emasculation of men—and here it has succeeded in spades.

Men are created to be the head of the community, to protect it, sacrifice for it, die for it if necessary. And to show you how bad things have become, stop and consider how much, even for a moment, that truth about men strikes you as a "sexist" statement. That's because for the past decades we have all had crammed into our psyches that men and women are the same.

No, we are not. But that's what we've been told. We are equal in dignity, certainly, but we are not the same in role. Sameness does not mean equality.

Ah, but the women's libbers, the demonic mouthpieces, were storming up and down the streets of San Francisco back in the halcyon days of the late '60s and early '70s burning their bras and demanding "equal rights." Their goal may have been one thing, but their master's goal was something else entirely. The women's lib philosophy became the bucket in which the satanic carried its philosophy into the culture at large.

Men and women were pitted against each other, with women portrayed as the victims and men as the oppressors—and the only answer to this was that women had to become more like men, psychologically, emotionally, even physically. With the injection of the contraceptive pill into the equation, it was lights out. Now women could have sex with no consequences (or so they were told, and were eager to believe). This attitude fed the worst instincts of men: sex with no responsibility. It was Eve handing Adam the fruit all over again.

But when you play to someone's lowest, basest inclinations, you are setting yourself on the short course to destruction. Men were now free to abandon their heroic calling and live in the muck of the Sexual Revolution. They could have as much intercourse as possible, and women were left holding the bag—or, more precisely, the baby—which they would then either kill or raise without a father.

Fatherless sons have a much more difficult time becoming men because there is no man to show them how to become a man, and boys will always stay boys unless a man drags them kicking and screaming out of adolescence. And if there is no man to drag them along, then the only remaining remedy is that some circumstance of life bites them where it hurts, that the roof comes crashing down on them, and then they are forced to grow up fast—things like falling in with the wrong crowd, ending up in jail, losing all sense of self-worth, pining after a father they never knew or had, developing addictions to drugs, alcohol, sex, pornography, and so forth.

Satan has a million tricks in his filthy bag and always seems to know exactly which one to pull out at the perfect time. Again, man can never outsmart a demon. So what has women's lib caused? Not so much the liberation of women, but the enslavement of men. How free are women these days forty years later? Poll after poll shows most would rather be at home nurturing their families than out in the daily work world pounding away and being ground up in the machine.

Many have to contend with troubled sons acting out, while holding down a job, having to wear not just the skirt but also the pants. All the while, men have been lowered to a degree that no previous culture even considered possible. Large segments of Western culture have been consumed by the effect of women's liberation not on women, but on men. Men have stayed boys, but in men's bodies—always a dangerous combination.

The very notion of masculinity has been turned on its head. The high ideals and beauty of masculinity have been swamped by the dark side of the masculine: a concentration on nothing but love of self. An entirely new male narcissism has been born, and its mother was women's lib. That singular irony alone reveals the hand of the diabolical in steering this ship.

For the world to be restored—and this includes most especially the Catholic Church—a true sense of the masculine must be restored. If the notion of father is left to twist in the wind, then the notion of God as Father can never be grasped. And that's exactly how Satan wants it.

All Things New: The Man Haters
Originally aired December 10, 2014

YOUNG MEN ARE BEING RAKED over the coals in this culture by the high-powered engines of radical feminism. The feminist extremists, which includes some men, and their "men are despicable" philosophy occupy the high ground in every institution, largely because they have played the victim card to perfection.

They control the education establishment, the media, the entertainment world, the courts, and even the various religious bodies—and they have done this by taking aim squarely at authentic masculinity. So today, older boys and younger men dance to the music of feminist rage, not to mention quite a few older males as well, who still knew better back in the bra-burning days of the 1960s.

The masculine has become so belittled and denigrated that boys do the easiest, laziest, most gratifying thing available and simply retreat into video games and pornography, and are drugged up by the feminazi-controlled education system, which diagnoses *one in seven* American boys as having Attention Deficit Hyperactivity Disorder and then writes them a script for Ritalin, a powerful mood stabilizer, for being nothing more than boys.

The scourge of the Church in the past fifty years has been the lack of the authentic masculine, because an effective authentic masculinity would never have allowed this highly charged, destructive, radical feminism to emerge and kill the men.

In December 2014, Hillary Clinton gave a speech at Georgetown. She strode up to the podium in her pantsuit and strongly suggested that women are better at foreign policy and governing than men. According to her, they're better at building coalitions and reaching consensus than men. Apparently, she's never heard of Queen Elizabeth I or Mao Tse Tung's wife.

During the University of Virginia frat rape story—which turned out to be much more fantasy than reality—the feministas were tripping all over themselves on TV outlets breathlessly denouncing men in high drama, again pushing the victim angle and saying women were objects of hate. So where are all the men? We see idiot men in TV commercials and sitcoms. We see serial killer men in movies. We see sex-crazed men in music videos, and we see effeminate men in religious realms.

But where are the real men? They've been sidelined because strong authentic men—meaning those who try and imitate Our Blessed Lord—are an obstacle to the weak, effeminate, emotion-saturated high dudgeon of radical feminism. And it is precisely this that must be fought against; shrill, radical feminism must be confronted by confident, authentic masculinity—which means it must be developed, coached up, and trained.

The two main weapons Satan has used superbly, has used in tandem with each other, is the media and the destroyed sense of the masculine. The counter-attack against the culture must be an all-out, daily, broad-based assault, and in order to accomplish that, there need to be shock troops, strong, unwavering, ready to dedicate themselves to the struggle. The battle is the spiritual warfare that must be fought, but also trained and prepared for.

Church Militant goes toe to toe every day with the culture of evil and radical feminism that have invaded the Church and laid waste to souls. Not only do we fight this, as many other faithful apostolates do, we have been blessed to be given the tools and know-how to broadcast the struggle and expose the lies of the enemy to many Catholics who would otherwise remain in the dark.

Fatherhood Model
Originally aired June 16, 2015

WHAT THE HEDONISTIC WORLD fails to understand
when it comes to manhood is that it is designed
specifically to be oriented toward fatherhood, whether bio-
logical or spiritual. The ultimate model for fatherhood is God
the Father.

This is one reason the call for "inclusive" language is such
folly. It ultimately denies or greatly downplays that God is
Father, that all masculinity takes its cue from God. The crazy
habit-burning, veil-burning nuns of the 1960s and onward
were so desperate to be like men that they set about to
redefine masculinity. They centered on the bad aspects of
masculinity, just as they ignored the good aspects of femininity, and turned the theological world on its head.

All of a sudden, being a man was bad: We were evil, mean,
oppressive, destroyers of women. Our part of the human
species had to be exposed for the lugs we are. It went from a
case of there being some bad men to "men are bad" to "the
masculine is bad" to "fatherhood, the object of masculinity, is
bad, unneeded." And the dark side of masculinity (and there
is one, just as there is with femininity) sat up and paid
attention.

When bad women got to define what manhood is, the wheels
came off. The dark side of the masculine was more than
willing to allow manhood to be classified as a bundle of sex
and violence and laziness. And it wasn't soon after that that
manhood was being portrayed for all the world to see as a
mish-mash of self-indulgence and dim intellect. Men, the
world has been told, are just a step above brutes, and all
they're interested in is sexual release, self-absorption, and
self-indulgence. Such a person can be roundly ignored, the
logic goes.

Of course, this projection is made onto God as well. He is a
self-absorbed male, the feminist thinking goes, a personality

Who can be ignored and dismissed and Who is too self-centered to be of any real significance in our lives. Once that construct is in place, it can now be projected throughout the universe. Colleges can begin Feminine Studies departments; the move to ordain women as priests can gain momentum; men's college athletics departments can have their budgets savaged by Title IX rules that demand equal funding for women's sports programs; women don't need a man to have a child, and children don't need a father.

And *that* is the brass ring right there: Children don't need a father because fatherhood is unimportant. And because fatherhood is unimportant, so is God. God has ordered His creation in such a way that the result of attacking or disfiguring a part of it results in a disfiguring of our perception of Him, the Creator. When fatherhood is maligned and short-changed, so is the image of God in us because the very nature of God is attacked.

God as Father defines the first order, the first place, the first dynamic of the life of the Trinity. There can be no Son without the Father. The entire mission of our Blessed Lord was to lead us to His Father. "[N]o one comes to the Father, but by me" (John 14:6). "No one can come to me unless the Father who sent me draws him" (John 6:44). "Thou art my Son, today I have begotten thee" (Hebrews 5:5).

All over the Old Testament the relationship between God and His chosen people is frequently described as that of a father to his children. But the hedonist world—and that includes the theological hedonists *inside* the Church—fail to grasp the fundamental reality: God is Father. They mouth the words—that is, when they aren't trying to change them—but they ignore their actual import: how the whole order of creation is based on the Fatherhood of God.

The destruction of the notion of fatherhood is ultimately an attack aimed at God, at the divine order created by Him. That is why the whole world has spun out of control, why homosexuality is so rampant, why men are surgically altering themselves to be woman-like, why families are in disarray, why so many men have lost almost all concept of the authentic masculine.

It all boils down to failing to understand that God is the model of all fatherhood. When a man grasps that, he will be well on the road to getting his children to Heaven—which is, of course, the entire reason God has shared His own paternity with him in the first place.

Who's Your Daddy?
Originally aired July 22, 2015

THE SLANG EXPRESSION "Who's your daddy?" holds
much significance these days owing to the "man crisis." A
boy passing into young manhood is at a severe disadvantage
without a father rooted in the Faith. That is so blindingly
clear it seems almost insulting to a person's intelligence even
to say it; but it must be said.

The lack of a good man in a boy's life is almost guaranteed to
bring a world of hurt for the boy—and not just in the usually
considered way. Of course the absence of a faith-filled father
will create a huge deficit in the boy's life. There are the rare
exceptions, of course, that a substitute dad in the form of a
grandfather or uncle or even a very involved coach can serve
as a good safety net, but those cases aren't the rule.

And the great disadvantage is this: Not only does a young
fellow not have a strong man to harness all that energy and
vinegar of youth and properly direct it, but he has a whole
world of horrible men out there willing to lead him down the
path of destruction. It isn't really a question of not having a
dad as much as it is the question *"Who* is your daddy?"

There are simply too many men waiting to devour young
impressionable boys. From Hollywood celebrities and entertainment industry icons, there are dozens of males who
substitute for a missing father. Instead of teaching boys how
to be men, they teach boys how to stay boys, self-absorbed
juveniles who gratify themselves with sex and video games.
But this eventually has the negative impact of building up
rage in boys as they mature into men. Somewhere down in
their spirit they feel the pain of rejection. This isn't the sad
case of a father dying. It's the even sadder case of a father
rejecting, actively rejecting his son, and the son knowing it on
some level and incorporating it into his self-perception. This
can inspire a self-loathing and anger and result in all kinds of
bad choices the boy is predisposed to make.

And we aren't talking about just physically absent fathers, but rather spiritually negligent fathers, those who do not pass on or instill the Faith in their children. They rob their child of spiritual security and youthful happiness. Right at the moment that a boy turns to look for his dad, in need of his Heavenly Dad, he often finds neither.

What a blow to his psyche and an even more shattering blow to his soul. The boy is now left to fend for himself and go in emotional search of his father—any father, if need be. Fueled by anger, a boy can accept any male as his father, figuratively more than literally. So he goes all in on the images of manhood that show violence, sex, drugs, alcohol—whatever seems to anesthetize the hurt. These things feed his anger more than subdue it. And the ability to go off the rails oftentimes becomes a reality.

The culture is more than happy to lay young men to waste, to abuse them by feeding the dark side of their innate mas-culinity, the destructive side. The culture cares nothing for young men except to profit from them or even exploit them. Boys need a father, a faith-filled man of God to love them deeply, who is there for them every day teaching them how to be self-sacrificing. Consider this: Even though strictly speaking He didn't *need* an earthly father, His Heavenly Father gave charge of Jesus to St. Joseph.

When the final curtain finishes dropping on Western civi-lization, one of the saddest lines of our history will be the anguished tale of boys who had no fathers to teach them about their Heavenly Father.

Chapter Nine

Liturgy

F OR THE OVERWHELMING NUMBER of Catholics, their primary if not sole touchstone to the Church is their local parish. And it is at the parish level where the Faith is lived—or killed. Judging from the massive numbers of desertions from the Faith, killed is the more likely of the two options. For every convert to the Catholic faith, six leave. One out of every eight Americans walking around is a former Catholic. In 2012, the number was one out of every ten.

In the 2008 U.S. presidential election, 25 percent of the electorate was Catholic; in the 2016 election the percentage had fallen to 21 percent. While a drop of 4 percent, however regrettable, may not seem all that worrisome, that 4-percent decrease in the overall number of Catholics relative to the U.S. population means that the Church lost 20 percent—one out of every five members—in just eight years.

This means something is happening in the parishes, aside from massive numbers closing. The parish closing and clustering epidemic is a further symptom that something is sick inside the standard Catholic parish. There are now fewer Catholic parishes in the United States than there were before 1965. The Church is going backwards.

And it is precisely going back that many people are beginning to realize needs to happen—back as in the liturgy, back to a more reverent, meaningful liturgy, as men like Pope Benedict have called for. The problem is, once again, the bishops. A majority of them do not want the Mass being celebrated in the extraordinary form (i.e., the Traditional Latin Mass), and to whatever degree they do allow it, it is often grudgingly and relegated to inconvenient neighborhoods at inconvenient times.

If the condition of the Church is a reflection of the condition of the faithful, which it is, then the condition of the faithful is a reflection of the condition of the liturgy. Until reverence is restored and preaching is fixed, nothing is turning around. The "mass" migration from the Church will continue.

Girl Altar Boys
Originally aired January 27, 2015

FROM TIME IMMEMORIAL, it has been males serving at the altar, not females. But the Church of Nice, which respects nothing but its own desires, has set about to overthrow that and pushed and promoted the French Revolution, the freemasonic folly of "equality," and concluded that—tradition be damned—we need "girl altar boys." That phrase "girl altar boys" sounded strange and awkward, so the gender-neutral phrase was introduced of altar "servers."

It may or may not be a cause of the continuing decline in correct Catholic self-identity, but it is one of the clarion calls around which the Church of Nice circles its wagons when the trumpet is sounded. The Church of Nice, anti-tradition firing squad gets all kinds of assistance from the secular crowd—which, of course, makes sense, since the Church of Nice is born of secular, worldly thought and not Catholic thought.

Case in point: San Francisco's Star of the Sea parish, where the pastor, Fr. Joseph Illo, declared in 2015 that the sanctuary would return to its centuries-old habitat for men; henceforward, all servers at the altar would be male. Altar boys only.

Ah, but the world and the Church of Nice didn't like this. This was a shining of the spotlight directly on the man-crisis in the Church, as Cdl. Raymond Burke, former prefect of the Apostolic Signatura, once said. To end the practice of "girl altar boys" overthrows every single heresy the Church of Nice worships. It destroys their notion that men and women are the same—not equal, but the same. It destroys their work to abolish the distinction between laity and ordained. It returns something of a sort of masculinity to the sanctuary, which, of course, the Church of Nice cannot stand.

The Church of Nice clergy and episcopate have done everything they can to convert the look and feel of Catholicism to a watered-down, protestantized sect. They've moved the tabernacle, practically hidden it; they've brought in horrible, sappy music; they've pushed for the reception of the Body and Blood of Our Lord in the hand; they've stuck a table in the sanctuary; they've obliterated the notion of sacrifice and substituted it with the plainness and boredom of just a meal; and, of course, they've invited girls into the sanctuary to continue the process.

The Mass especially has been assaulted in its appearance and practices and abuses because this is the place where most Catholics who still think they are Catholic experience the Faith. They put in their Sunday duty, grab their bulletin, and bolt out the door. So if that experience can be polluted and defiled and made to look and feel as not authentically Catholic, then all the better. Little by little, more and more Catholics will be made to feel less and less Catholic. And "girl altar boys" have always been just one more arrow in the quiver of the Church of Nice.

So for Fr. Illo to take this step was stupendous. And he had the backing not only of his archbishop, the stalwart Salvatore Cordileone of San Francisco, but also the Vatican. As recently as 2001, the Congregation for Divine Worship, under whose jurisdiction this issue of "girl altar boys" falls, stated clearly that while an individual bishop can permit the practice, he is under no obligation to allow it, regardless of what his particular national conference may have to say about the matter.

So while a local bishop may give the practice of "girl altar boys" the green light, no priest may be forced to employ them, a bishop may not force a pastor to accept the practice, and there is in fact an obligation to support the practice of altar boys. That is quite the statement from Rome. In short, a bishop may make this ill-advised decision to permit female servers if he wants, but he can't force it down the throats of his priests. The norm—the usual, accepted, preferred, desired, longed-for intention and wish of the Church—is for male-only altar servers. Allowing female servers is an aberration, a side show.

But this longing on the part of the Church did not prevent the Church of Nice gang from going after Fr. Joseph Illo and Star of the Sea parish. The predictions came that the parish would go bankrupt because of its allegedly chauvinistic, sexist, misogynistic, paternal pastor and his "hatred" toward women. The local CBS TV station in San Francisco actually sent a reporter to do a live shot on this story, believe it or not. Talk about a slow news day.

Church Militant set up a fundraising site for Catholics to show their support for Fr. Illo and his embattled parish. In a short amount of time, we raised $50,000 for the church—which, as of the time of this writing, continues to flourish. The financial support that poured in from the faithful from all over the country was a direct slap in the face to the Church of Nice, and an encouragement to other priests wishing to restore traditional liturgy and reinforce authentic Catholic identity in their parishes.

It is crucial that Catholic faithful show support to good priests, spiritually, morally, financially. It's in winning small battles like these that will lead to winning the war against inauthentic, destructive, Church of Nice Catholicism.

Saint Judas
Originally aired May 1, 2015

WHEN WE SPEAK OF THE CHURCH OF NICE, we mean the institutional approach laid out and backed by weak, feminized male leaders who do not want to preach the hard truths of the Faith. Why they don't want to is based on many motives we've already covered numerous times.

At the heart of the Church of Nice is an accommodationist attitude that refuses to deal in the supernatural reality preached by Our Blessed Lord that humans go to Hell. He Himself tells us this directly in Matthew's Gospel. These people, clergy and laity, have for decades downplayed Hell— the consequence of unrepented mortal sin—and this approach has spun off all kinds of ills in the Church.

When Hell is ignored, then so is sin, because, simply put, if there's no serious chance of going to Hell, then sin doesn't really have any serious consequence beyond this life. If there's no sin, there's no real need for the sacrament of confession, because what exactly would you be confessing? And why would you be confessing it? If the sacrament of confession is unneeded, deemed not a necessity, then there's no real reason to worry all that much about people in a state of mortal sin receiving Holy Communion, or for that matter, even non-Catholics.

In fact, since the disposition of one's soul is an immaterial consideration, then it also follows that the teaching that the Blessed Sacrament is the Body, Blood, Soul, and Divinity of Jesus Christ, really, truly, and substantially present under the appearance of bread and wine, doesn't really matter that much. After all, if the point of reception of Holy Communion is to join oneself to Our Blessed Lord to increase in sanctity and prepare for full communion with Him in the next life—if Hell is not a serious consideration, then it doesn't really matter what state our souls are in, because there are no serious everlasting consequences for living in sin. And if the sacraments of penance and Holy Communion are not all that serious, then it naturally follows that the priesthood, which is how these sacraments are conferred on the laity, isn't all that important, either.

Do you see what ignoring Hell does, the impact it has? It empties the confessionals, obliterates the need to be properly disposed to receive the Body and Blood of Our Lord, and reduces the dignity and necessity of the priesthood by blurring the line between the ordained and non-ordained (and more than blurring, simply erases). This is why the Mass has taken on the character of an assembly of people getting together on a Sunday to hang out and sing some bad hymns off-key while we go up and eat our "piece of bread," which is how so many see it, even though it is still the Body and Blood or Our Lord, which we get from the sloppily attired, post-menopausal woman on our way to the mall without having considered our own unworthiness.

Erase Hell and you erase the need for the Church, which is to defeat the gates of Hell in the life of each person.

Judas is the patron saint of the Church of Nice. And the one thing to bear in mind is that this evil adopted by so many in the Church, including vast swaths of the clergy and even bishops, comes to us by way of the Protestant heresy, courtesy of Protestant theologian Karl Barth. Barth is practically worshiped in the hoity-toity crowd of Catholic eggheads who have high IQs but are woefully deficient in wisdom.

One of them was Catholic theologian Hans Urs von Balthasar, who came up with the massively un-Catholic idea that "we have a reasonable hope that all men are saved"—including Judas. His error has been spread by popular leaders like Bp. Robert Barron, who once ran the seminary for the arch-diocese of Chicago and is now auxiliary bishop in Los Angeles, instilling this Protestant-heresy inspired notion into the minds of the flock in his charge.

His flock would be better served by reading the works and thoughts of St. Thomas Aquinas and St. Augustine, whom Bp. Barron has smilingly dismissed as too severe on the subject of Hell. Too severe? Those Doctors of the Church are echoing the words of Our Blessed Lord Himself. Is God too severe on this point for the Church of Nice?

The answer is, sadly, yes. The Church of Nice thinks that all this Hell business is a little over the top. That's why they can't have a serious, take-no-prisoners discussion about it. It's why it's never in their homilies. It's why they tell starving souls in confession that this isn't a sin and that isn't a sin. It's why they celebrate Mass with the decorum of a boring circus. It's why they drone on and on about mercy, when what they're really offering is a false compassion, a false understanding of mercy.

They have erected their own belief system and taken the label "Catholic" because they have kept the buildings and institutions and, to all outward appearances, it's Catholic. But at its heart, it isn't Catholic. The importance of the sacraments is shunted off, the theology is accommodated to feelings and emotions, the liturgy is minimalized and made a mockery of.

The liturgy in particular has been most offended against in this great whitewash of Hell. The Mass involves being present to and at the great Sacrifice of God the Son to God the Father on our behalf. It is the Sacrifice of the Mass, the unbloody representing of Calvary. It is the cause of our redemption.

But since the idea of redemption and salvation are thrown overboard in the whitewashing of Hell, then the purpose of the Mass shifts, from one of sacrifice (because there is no real need for a sacrifice) to a gathering of the assembly, where we, the Church, are the most important aspect of the event. So the homilies have to shift, the music has to shift, the very direction the priest faces has to shift, the occupants of the sanctuary need to shift, the people who administer Holy Communion need to shift—all these need to shift from reflecting the notion of sacrifice to the protestant notion that it's the people who matter.

This is why there is such tremendous blowback from notable Church leaders, in private and in public, about the Mass being offered in Latin, for example. They want nothing to upset the carefully planted idea in people's minds, installed by errant theologians, that the Mass is really about we the people gathering around a table for some food. Imagine what would happen if a priest in a run-of-the-mill parish in a run-of-the-mill diocese started offering Mass the way it was envisioned by the fathers of the Second Vatican Council and faced the same direction as the people, meaning toward God. The Church of Nice would quickly see a demonstration of Hell, because all Hell would break loose with the bishop and scores of local priests—all because Fr. Smith just wanted to do what the Council said he should do.

Greed and disobedience are what led to Judas Iscariot's damnation, and unless it's repented of, it's what will lead to the damnation of the Church of Nice as well. Too much of Catholic identity is at stake to keep silent on this matter of Hell, sin, and Judas any longer.

Megachurch Mentality
Originally aired December 11, 2015

WHEN, IF EVER, will Catholic leaders in America get through their thick skulls that we need to stop imitating protestant garbage in our churches? Not just the watered-down faith, which is mostly *du jour* every Sunday, but the constant megachurch mentality? Big screens, sickeningly friendly worship "ministers," youth bands, laser shows, dancing, hand-holding, that awful, syrupy, St. Louis, homosexual, Jesuit, protestant-inspired "music," and so forth.

The Catholic Church has the fullness of the truth, the King of the Universe on our altars and in our tabernacles—and we spend all this time trying to Madison Avenue our way down the aisle. What is wrong with our leaders?

The lack of concern for the flock for the past fifty years has left them vulnerable to looking around for a "religious experience" that is "meaningful." They want God, but they have been conditioned by the larger protestant worldview of looking for God to look not for God but for an experience, a feeling. When they have a feeling, they equate it with God, the Holy Spirit, whatever.

And so we have the phenomenon of the megachurch, where thousands of lost souls gather each week in great big auditoriums being overstimulated by preachers who are off the mark, with loud music, big productions, and sensory overload. It is the most emotional experience of the week for them, and in their misguided minds, they think it's God moving them.

Many Catholics haunt these halls because they were deprived of the truth years ago by lazy, cowardly, or wicked bishops and their equally vacuous clergy, and in the absence of intellectual stimulation and truth, they went in search of something to fill up their souls. And what is most galling of all now is that, as Catholics see their numbers falling, weakminded leaders, without a clue about how to read the signs of the times, want to imitate the megachurch model. They have fallen into the mentality that these rock-and-roll religious refugees are jammed to the rafters, so let's do what they do.

What they are not paying attention to, however, is what is going on just beneath the surface of this apparent success. A new study, done every five years by the Beck Group and which traces the success of megachurch Protestantism, suggests things are not so wonderful in la-la land as they appear.

While the number of worship centers has increased, and the number of people on the rolls at more than 70 percent of those worship centers has increased, the number of people who show up each week is on the decline. And that means the emotional thrill ride is coming to an end for an increasing number of churchgoers. Weekly attendance at these mega-churches has dipped precipitously. Two statistics bear this out.

While the number of worship centers has increased in the past five years—meaning there are more buildings—the number of people in those buildings each week has dropped by 30 percent since 2009. That means the overall numbers of megachurch attendees are not increasing but just spreading themselves out over more megachurches.

And at each megachurch, on average, the number of people who attend per week compared to the total number of people on the rolls is down from 96 percent to 82 percent in the past five years. The emotion overdrive is beginning to peter out, in other words. And that's to be expected. Why wouldn't it? People aren't built to be driven from one emotion-crazed overload to another—which makes it so curious that Catholic leaders seem to think this is the way to go: more emotion, more stimulation, more jokes, more relevance, more laser light shows.

God is not found in these religious hot houses. He's found in the depth of Catholicism, the Faith of the ages, properly and beautifully explained in all its glory and sublime truth. People were created for Catholicism; it's in their bones, not in these

Hollywood side shows and drum-banging contests. Those things answer people's psychologies and emotions. The Faith answers their deepest needs.

All of this must be fought: false religions, the false ideas and preachings that fall from false religions, most especially the false ideas that have worked themselves into the Catholic Church. We must resist these ferociously and defeat them. And the people who must fight it are the people who know the truth.

Hating on Tradition
Originally aired January 5 2016

THERE ARE LEADERS IN THE CHURCH, many of them in influential posts, who simply do not like the traditions of the Catholic Church. And the degree of that dislike ranges from one based on lack of experience or exposure all the way up to abhorrence of the traditions and the desire to wipe out all vestiges of them from living memory.

This is not a new phenomenon. It's only new in the sense that some Catholics are beginning to recognize it. But it's been going on for a long time now, so much so that it's a safe bet many Catholics are almost entirely unaware of Catholicism expressed in its traditions. The Faith as it was lived and experienced by the saints looks odd to newcomers.

Think about that for a moment; let that sink in. The Catholic Church in Her traditional expression is not recognized by many of Her children—a Mother whose children suffer from a horrible case of spiritual amnesia. This includes many converts to the Faith: well-intentioned Protestants who know nothing of the traditional expressions of the Faith because the vast majority of the lived Catholic experience today, including many of the luminaries, are not all that plugged into the Catholic faith as it was expressed for 1,500 years.

There are many and varied areas we can look at to see proof of this. It makes the most sense to begin with the Mass, because that is most Catholics' usual place of encounter with the Faith. The Mass as experienced by most Catholics today bears little outward resemblance to anything of Catholi-cism expressed traditionally. Pick almost anything in the Mass—at least as regards its outward expressions—and that expression is much more protestant than Catholic.

Hymns, a protestant development to supplant Gregorian chant, have been completely embraced to the detriment of chant. This is not to blow up hymns—many of them are quite wondrous—but their adoption by the Church was never intended to replace chant, which is purely Catholic. And while on the subject of music, even though the Church adopted some hymn use in the liturgy, the hymns She did permit were not rife with theological errors or almost completely man-centered, like many are today.

"Girl altar boys"—another novelty that isn't Catholic in any way. The opening of the sanctuary to women was another accommodation to modernism and flies in the face of authentic Catholic tradition. The priest turning his back to God so he can face the people, instead of leading them; that's another protestant novelty that isn't an expression of Catholic tradition. And it's one reason you now hear an ever-growing chorus of Church leaders like Cdl. Robert Sarah saying this needs to be done away with and the traditional mode re-established.

Holy Communion in the hand—*not* Catholic. To those who claim it was practiced in the Early Church, they fail to take into account that the Church learned from the experience, and that when Holy Communion is given in the hand, reverence for the Blessed Sacrament plummets, so the Church put an end to the practice.

Receiving from the chalice—that's another aberration introduced in the mid-twentieth century, like reception in the hand. The Protestant revolutionaries were keen at the beginning of their revolt to reduce the significance and importance of the Blessed Sacrament and the emphasis placed on it by that group of newly minted Protestants who had grown up as Catholics. So they watered things down for those first couple of generations in the sixteenth century until Holy Communion began to lose any sense of reverence, until the people began to see it as just a nice symbol.

And speaking of watering down the importance of Catholic traditions, so-called eucharistic ministers— absolutely and totally as un-Catholic as you can get. But the logic follows: If you can have those receiving Holy Communion handle it and become so familiar with it that they lose all sense of reverence, then why not do the same with those who distribute Holy Communion? Having lay people run to the tabernacle, take out the ciboria, handle the Sacred Species—all of this breaks down the distinction between priest and layman.

The priesthood is *Catholic*, a continuation of the priesthood from the Old Testament realized in the New Israel, the Catholic Church. It's hard to get more traditional than the priesthood, set aside for offering sacrifice and forgiveness of sins. So in the Church of Nice, that's another traditional expression that has to go. Stop calling them priest; call them "presider" instead—a truly silly term.

Holding hands at the "Our Father"—again, not Catholic. That's a pentecostal aberration allowed in by those who want anything and everything that bespeaks traditional expressions of Catholicism tossed out.

And this is just a partial list from just one area of the life of the Church. There are quite a few more in this area, as well as from many other areas. The tradition-haters use two primary modes of attack to eradicate tradition. They simply put an end to traditional expressions of Catholicism while at the same time introducing all kinds of novel things that aren't Catholic into the life of the Church, liturgy and otherwise.

The point is: Influential men in the Church today do not like tradition and traditional expressions of the Faith because those traditions—from chant to liturgical practices to devotions to the wording of prayers, all of it—they are each and all expressions of the *teachings* of the Church, Her beliefs, and *those* are what they want abolished or retooled.

They do not like the traditions because the traditions carry within themselves sensual expressions of the authentic faith. You can see, touch, taste, hear, and smell the truths of the teachings of the Faith in the Church's traditional practices, devotions, and expressions. The smell of incense, for example, and its use in the Mass is a reminder of the incense used in the Temple of Heaven, its sweet scent and odor something the demons themselves cannot long bear to endure because it brings to mind their fall. The touch of holy water on your hands and sprinkled on you brings to mind the waters of your baptism and our admission into the Church after having been claimed from Satan and remade into a son of God.

All, every one of them, every single traditional expression of the Faith, is rooted in the glory of Heaven, or a reminder of the spiritual warfare, the combat we are all called to wage every day we are alive. But this is not what the tradition-haters want you thinking about. They want your thoughts not focused on Heaven but on earth.

No Communion in the Hand
Originally aired March 9, 2016

THE PRIEST NEEDS TO STOP facing the people at Mass, and the destructive practice of giving Holy Communion in the hand needs to end. These two things, simple to do, would go a long way in fixing much that is wrong in the Church these days.

They were implemented by men in the 1960s and 1970s who wanted to refashion Catholic identity and make it more appealing to non-Catholics. Both practices have proven disastrous for the Church. So stop going down the wrong road, turn around, and get on the right one. The moves could be accompanied by correct catechesis and instruction on why this is being done. In that way, such moves would stand in direct contrast to the time when the horrible practices were instituted in the first place.

Like many watching and listening, I was alive when these things happened in my parish. I was an altar boy. We received practically no warning of these changes. One Sunday, without warning, a "table" appeared in the sanctuary. Our parish priests were smiling at the people awkwardly, and the people just smiled back. Not long after, we were told we could now come forward, stick out our hands, and "get" Holy Communion that way. This was in the diocese of Sacramento, California, run by a string of extremely liberal bishops going back to the 1960s.

But that was the case in many dioceses. They made sure their seminarians were taught to face the people and not God and then plop God in their hands. We would do away with kneeling and having the Sacred Host placed on our tongues because we were "mature" adults in the Faith, and mature adults stand.

Apparently, the liberal bishops forgot that Our Blessed Lord said, "Truly, I say to you, unless you turn and become like children, you will never enter the kingdom of heaven" (Matthew 18:3). This practice of receiving Holy Communion in the hand standing is wrong. It completely sends the wrong message and has contributed to a mass falling-away from the One True Faith.

This was done to accommodate protestant error. It should never have happened. It was done underhandedly by a cabal of duplicitous bishops led by, of course, Cdl. Joseph Bernardin of Chicago, one of the most influential prelates in the United States who did more to harm the Faith than many. This cabal illegally rammed through Communion in the hand and lied about it to officials in the Vatican in order to secure it—which the Vatican naïvely did.

Catholics simply need to stop participating in this horrid practice. And never let a priest tell you that you cannot receive on the tongue. That priest is wrong. Rome has said clearly that Catholics may receive on their knees and on their tongue—moreover, that this is the Church-preferred way to receive. Both practices are not equal. One is bad practice that is allowed; the other is what the Church *desires*.

You will be told you are showing off, trying to draw attention to yourself, disobeying the will of the bishop, disrupting unity. You will be told this was the way it was done back in the 300s. What you will *not* be told is that Holy Communion was not distributed in the hand in the fashion it is today, nor will you be told that the Church stopped that practice after it became apparent that lack of reverence for the Blessed Sacrament was becoming widespread.

Depending on where you go to Mass, you may be the only person who changes and begins to do this, and that's okay. It might make you feel funny, you might get noticed, the priest may say something to you. Do the better thing and receive your King on your knees and on the tongue. None of the rest matters.

What matters is resisting the garbage in the Church every-where you can and doing it immediately. Forget about the insults and slurs and "corrections" that will come your way, and simply kneel down before your King. And if you are a "eucharistic minister" (a misnomer), you need to resign from that abused position immediately.

There isn't much the laity can do in the practical realm to resist the evil that's been injected into the life of the Church, but this certainly is one way.

Chapter Ten

Media

THE MOST POTENT WEAPON the Demon has been able to manipulate has been the media, both entertainment and news, and all types: television, radio, film, newspaper, publishing, billboards, and so on. So pervasive is the diabolical in the realm of the media that Servant of God Fr. John Hardon called the monolith the "Luciferian Media." And so it is.

The media is controlled by the godless. Until that fact is accepted, no other discussion is possible. In particular, the poison combo of news and entertainment has proven to be most lethal. Both of these are simply different branches on the same tree. One is meant to deaden your intellect, while the other's aim is to arouse the passions.

When man was in Paradise, the passions were in complete subordination to the intellect. Man's inner core was completely ordered. But after the Fall, the situation reversed. Man's intellect was now overwhelmed by his passions. In point of fact, the goal of the Christian life can be summed up as the intense struggle, the combat of striving to restore the intellect to its superiority over the passions, a goal that most of humanity will never achieve.

The media plays on this struggle, wittingly or unwittingly, pressing its case a thousand times a day, every day, to have the passions remain in control and the intellect die a slow death.

The Drum Beat
Originally aired January 31, 2013

THE CATHOLIC CHURCH is having such a difficult time these days fighting evil, error, heresy, and dissent because all of these are constantly pounding the drum, the steady, never-ending bang, bang, bang of the drum.

It never stops. *Gay marriage is good. Homosexual rights are human rights. Abortion is a fundamental right. Contraception reduces unwanted pregnancies. Euthanasia helps people die with dignity.* Those are the bangs pounded out on the moral drum. On the theological drum, the beat goes on. *All religions are basically the same. There is no Hell—or if there is, no one is actually in it. Women should be priests. Non-Catholics can receive Holy Communion. Everyone goes to Heaven.*

Bang, bang, bang. It never stops. Never. This is the secret to evil's success in our days. And part of that drumbeat is what's not said, or what's distorted—like 650,000 pro-life marchers slogging up Constitution Avenue in the freezing cold, and the media treats it as though it never happened. They do this every year, year in, year out, for forty years. *Bang, bang, bang.*

It never ends. It's understandable that when anyone in America is exposed to the ceaseless banging of the drum, he might eventually come to believe the rhythm and the tune being banged out because he never hears anything else. How can it reasonably be expected that in the face of a media behemoth, with Super Bowl halftime shows that elevate humans to the level of deities, with TV programs that knit sexual deviancy into the fabric of normal life, where immorality is celebrated, where songs and their lyrics pollute young and old minds alike—in the face of all this, what else can be expected?

This is why the collapse of the Church, which is called to face these evils down and strike up its own beat, has been so devastating. Where is Church leadership on contraception? Where is the announcement from the U.S. bishops on a new plan to fight back against the evil, to go on the offensive in every Catholic parish in America? Where is the Catholic drumbeat *every day*? Does anyone seriously think that the lukewarm or easily intimidated are going to be able to stand firm in the face of the fierce winds that blow twenty-four hours a day, seven days a week, armed with little more than a drab, meaningless, seven-minute, once-a-week homily that says next to nothing?

Do the math. There are 168 hours in a week. Let's say you sleep eight hours a day. That leaves 112 hours—112 hours of exposure to posters in shopping malls, lewd jokes on TV or the radio, immorality on the internet, sexualized billboards on the freeway, immodest shots of cheerleaders for professional sports teams, sitcoms with sexual immorality as the running plot, movies glorifying illicit sex, major corporations financing sexual license, newspaper headlines mocking all things traditional . . .

And then when you turn to Church life, you run into a virtual cornucopia of confusing signals and counter-messages: pro-abortion Catholic politicians left alone, university theology departments cranking out heresy or dissent, priests doing worse, bishops remaining silent, taking the long-game approach, Holy Communion in the hand, kneeling being discouraged, altar girls, holding hands during the "Our Father," the sign of peace turning into a virtual love-in, LGBT Masses, parish council members and lay leaders using and supporting contraception, Catholic Obama supporters, and so on.

How on earth could anyone in his right mind expect that with all this nonsense—both outside and inside the Church—anyone could emerge from the 112 hours of this unending drumbeat week after week and think a few minutes at Mass each Sunday could counter this—and that's only for the 20 percent of Catholics who still go?

Where is the ceaseless Catholic drumbanging? Spending $10 million on a wonderful travelogue documentary is splendid. Dumping tons of money into a TV ad campaign is great, noble, well-intended—but don't expect the needle to move one bit because of it. Even if a few souls are recaptured, many more will have continued to slip through the cracks and be lost because of the non-stop drumbeat of evil.

This is why Church leaders must reorient their thinking, their strategy. If it isn't painfully obvious by now, whatever the strategy is, if there actually is a strategy, it isn't working. And it isn't working because the hit-and-miss approach of a great big World Youth Day, or Fortnight for Freedom, or whatever momentary flash, is just that—a flash in the pan. Church leaders have failed to understand the most basic concept of marketing in the modern world: saturation bombing, the steady drumbeat is what works—not the occasional big explosion that gets headlines (and sometimes they don't even get that).

It's the primary reason Church Militant gets out Catholic content every day, day in, day out, multiple times a day. We are at least trying to compete with the never-ending drumbeat of evil by pounding out the drumbeat for good. The media knows the power of saturation bombing. It's why they beat a story to death, repeat something over and over and over, stay on message regardless of obstacles, and never stop pounding and banging that drum.

But there's the difference: The media—movies, plays, TV, books, magazines, internet—stays on message. They are unified and aligned against truth. But for the Faith that possesses the fullness of truth, the Catholic Church, there is simply too much division; too much dissent within the ranks has been allowed to form and foment.

The Church can't preach a message each and every day with force and non-stop pounding against Hell, for example, because many of her own ministers reject the concept, at least on a practical level. Contraception? Who cares? Cohabitation? Gotta' get with the times—*wink, wink, nod, nod.*

As long as this is allowed to prevail—and that means bishops who are allowing it because no one else has the power to change it—there will never be a unified message. And if there is no unified message, then there can never be the consistent *bang, bang, bang* of the drum to counter the drumbeat of evil. Just don't be surprised, Bishops, when you wake up one day and can't understand why the noise is so loud that your cathedrals have rattled off their foundations and fallen to the ground.

Gullible Catholics
Originally aired April 15, 2015

THERE'S SOMETHING TO BE SAID for generally good news, and then something to be said for keeping that news in perspective. If someone hands you $100, that's good news. If you owe $100,000, the $100 is still good news, but from the perspective of your debt, you don't go wild with happiness.

But that's what a lot of the Church of Nice crowd did in reaction to news from the U.S. bishops' conference about the number of newly ordained priests in America in 2015. The Church of Nice blogs and even some more usually reliable Catholic media popped open champagne corks and celebrated one isolated report as though it were the best piece of news ever reported.

A little perspective, please.

First, the news was that there had been a 25-percent increase in the number of priestly ordinations in the United States over the previous year. 2015 had 595 ordinations; 2014 had 494—about a hundred more ordinations than the year before. That's good news as it stands. And faithful Catholics are always grateful for their priests. That's not the point. What is the point is the out-of-proportion reaction to the news. And it is out of proportion precisely because it lacks context or perspective.

Before we examine the news in context, let's examine the reasons for the near-hysterical joy. First, the Church of Nice crowd is desperate to report anything that makes it look as though the Church of Nice approach is successful. So they blow up the social media world and the blogs with headlines like "Huge Jump in New Ordinations!" That kind of headline and internet chatter, they think, provides justification for their constant excuse-baiting about the crisis in the Church.

The party line goes something like this: *See! There's no crisis. A huge jump in ordinations! Don't listen to all those doomsayers like*

Church Militant and other Catholic independent media sources.

For faithful Catholics, headlines like this can serve as something of a panacea, can provide a much-desired reason to think that things are turning around. The Church of Nice trumpets the headlines because the story serves as cover for their constant denial of the crisis. Less-informed faithful yet desperate Catholics get some relief. Both sides are wrong because the context is not reported by the Church of Nice and not sought after by the faithful crowd, anxiety-ridden to hear any good news at all.

Now for the context, the perspective. A 25-percent jump in new priestly ordinations is of course good news. But it isn't the first time it's happened. In 2006–2007, there was another 25-percent jump: from 359 to 475. So this is hardly anything new, however welcome it may be. That 475 number of newly ordained from 2007 has remained pretty constant, with a few variations here and there, until 2015, which had the number up to 595.

As for the raw number of 595, again, it's good news, but put the corks back in the bottles. That was the number of priests newly ordained in 1990—twenty-five years earlier. So what exactly is being celebrated here, that we are now back to the future with the same number of new priests from a quarter century earlier?

And if you go back even further in time, say, thirty years before that, all the way back to 1965—that year there were almost 1,000 priests ordained in the United States. So all these Church of Nice excuse-makers need to shut down their blogs and get a clue. (By the way, all these numbers are from the U.S. bishops conference's own reports.)

Additionally, if you look at the ratio of priests to the overall Catholic population, the news is actually horrible. Going on the U.S. bishops' own numbers, in 1965, there were 46 million Catholics, and 1,000 newly ordained priests emerged from those 46 million. In 2015, there are 66 million Catholics, and only 595 newly ordained priests emerged from those 66 million. While the Catholic population has grown along with the overall population by about 30 percent, the number of newly ordained has shrunk by roughly 40 percent.

What should be happening with an overall increase in Catholic population is a corresponding overall increase in the number of new ordinations. Going on the 1965 number of 1,000 new priests out of 46 million Catholics, in 2015 there correspondingly should have been 1,300 new priests ordained. But there were less than half—only 595.

To trumpet a headline without digging more deeply is irresponsible, reckless, misleading, and possibly even deceitful. The truth is what matters, not calming fears or advancing an agenda riddled with falsities. And when you look further into this Pollyanna-ish world of "reporting," the news is even worse. The reception of every single sacrament that records are kept for—except this very slight increase in ordinations—is at historic lows.

Baptisms of infants, minors, and adults—all three categories—are down year after year to now record lows, and are off by more than a whopping 50 percent compared to 1965. Confirmations are down by 10 percent since 1990 and falling every year in that twenty-five-year span. First Communions are down by more than 10 percent since 1990 and are lower in almost every year in that twenty-five-year span.

Perhaps most frightening of all, Catholic marriages have simply fallen off the cliff. There are nearly 60 percent fewer marriages compared to 1965, and the drop-off has continued nearly every year since. This is the one perhaps most disturbing trend because it portends the most significance looking into the future. Dramatically fewer Catholic couples—350,000 in 1965, down to only 150,000 in 2015—means a huge drop-off in the number of Catholic families in the immediate future and a much smaller pool of potential priests in the medium- to long-term future. And again, all these numbers are torn right from the U.S. bishops' own reports.

So, yes be happy about 100 more priestly ordinations compared to the previous year. But don't be foolish about it, as the Church of Nice crowd likes to be because it's their nature. There is no significant turnaround going on in the Church, and by any human measure, it's going to get a lot worse in the near future.

Supernatural, superhuman effort is needed because the situation calls for it, not Pollyanna hoping and Church of Nice excuse-making. This situation is beyond critical. The Faith has been and is still being betrayed by poorly formed clergy, homosexual clergy, poorly educated laity in positions of authority in chanceries and schools, many of whom disagree with the Magisterium in their lives and in their words.

The reality is this: There is only a very small percentage of faithful Catholics among the clergy and laity, and until this reality is accepted and a plan of action implemented to attack the causes, nothing is going to change. Stop celebrating a small victory in battle as though the enemy has been defeated. It's silly and unbecoming of serious Catholics who understand what's really at stake.

Money, Media, Message, Movement
Originally aired May 26, 2015

THERE IS SO MUCH CONFUSION in the Church these days it tears your heart out. The confusion leads to division as people, good Catholics, fall overboard trying to navigate their way in the midst of a typhoon of evil.

In the meantime, the other side, the dark side, continues to consolidate its power and strengthen its hand. It plays a sophisticated game, taking its ideology, pouring tons of money behind it so they can market the message effectively in the mass media, thereby making a movement that generates its own media, attracts more money—and the cycle continues until a sufficient number of people have been convinced the movement is right.

We call this cycle the four M's: Money, Media, Message, Movement. It has proven enormously effective, and it's one that Catholics need to start employing. The means of creating a movement is the media, both news and entertainment media. Print media has been used effectively, but when the electronic media came online, it quickly became dominant.

But media is expensive, and the evil-minded people pushing these agendas of sodomite marriage, contraception, abortion, and so forth know this. As a result, they have directed large shares of their fortune toward media efforts, because they know the average person is so easily influenced by media messaging. This is why candidates for the presidency spend upwards of $1 billion on their campaigns. *Huge* portions of that money are used on TV commercials.

The reason this strategy is so effective is because it is based on one underlying assumption: that people are lacking in information and will not care enough, owing to their lack of information, to go seek out the truth. They will simply take what is offered to them and assimilate it into their thoughts, and eventually their lives and voting patterns.

This is what happened in Ireland with the 2015 gay marriage

vote, and earlier in the United States with divorce and contraception. All over the former countries of Christendom, evil-minded people—with Satan as their unseen commander—overthrew nearly 2,000 years of understanding and order in less than fifty years because the media could be used so effectively to capitalize on people's ignorance and indifference.

People need to be re-educated. There has been a renaissance of sorts in political circles using the electronic media, with numerous conservative political commentators with large followings. But these have proven insufficient to turn the tide. They may have somewhat slowed it, but they will not be able to carry the day.

That's because they do not preach and teach to save souls, but to establish a certain political point of view. Granted, that point of view is far superior to the current status quo, but it is still flawed. It is flawed—as anything is—because it does not admit Catholic truth in its entirety. While there are some good things and good points in their idealized Americana version of society, again, America is not the world's salvation. The Catholic Church is the only one that can lay claim to that truth.

In fact, there is a danger among certain groups of Catholics today to look to the political order for the salvation of the culture. In the end, they will be frustrated. The only way ultimately to save the culture is to convert it to truth in its entirety—which is to say, Catholicism. That *must* be the goal, and because of that, we here at Church Militant consider that we have as our marching orders to go out and baptize all nations.

The ideology is saving souls by shining the light of Catholic truth on them. We do that by using the media of the internet to spread the message and help create a movement, an apostolic movement dedicated to spreading Catholic truth and fighting the powers of Hell. In short, we fight Hell's fire with fire. We give Hell a taste of its own medicine. When we were reading about the behind-the-scenes tactics engaged in by Atlantic Philanthropies to get Ireland to accept sodomite marriage, and America to accept Obamacare, let's just say it's tough not to get mad.

We need to fight back, and we need to wake other Catholics up to the fact that we need to fight back. At this moment, that is the biggest battle we all have. We need to be relentless in educating people to these dangers, just as the other side was relentless in flipping the culture. We need to be relentless in flipping back what we can.

Tsk, Tsk, CRS!
Originally aired June 5, 2015

C AN THERE BE ANY DOUBT LEFT that the word "Catholic" needs to disappear from the entity called Catholic Relief Services (CRS)? This charade that they are Catholic has long outlasted its usefulness. It's now just foolish. CRS is about as Catholic as the local Saul Alinsky Community Organizing Club renting space at Democratic Party headquarters.

In April 2015, Church Militant reported that the outfit's Vice President for Overseas Finance, Rick Estridge, was an out-and-proud homosexual *and* had gotten civilly married to his male partner. We even showed the marriage license from public records to make the point (not that anyone at "Catholic" Relief Services would have dared deny it). Estridge not only had pictures all over his desk broadcasting his homosexuality, but he was also all over social media with it, and blasting traditional family groups in the process.

Six weeks after the uproar began, it shifted gears. Estridge resigned following the scandal, and CRS went postal. In a statement on its site, the Catholic charity first comes to Estridge's defense as though he is a victim (because, of course, militant homosexuals are *always* the victim). Then CRS turns on faithful Catholics for having the supposed lack of charity to post the story and report the news.

Don't Catholics being petitioned to financially support a supposedly Catholic outfit that hires same-sex married people have a right to know? We think they do. And most faithful Catholics would agree with us.

We are being asked by this group, cajoled by numerous bishops throughout the country, to give *our* money to "Catholic" Relief Services. The group gets hundreds of millions of dollars from the federal government to supposedly fight poverty and go around the world fighting injustice—but at the same time, it directly contributes to that evil by spreading contraception and sterilization by funding local

Third-World groups that carry out the work. Then CRS cries foul when it gets caught, refuses to address any details of the actual facts, and turns around and hammers its critics, calling them names—a typical Saul Alinksy-type tactic, by the way, picked up on by the social justice, liberal elites.

But sometimes, those stories are a little hard to follow. You have to concentrate on them because they are in far-off lands, there are a thousand acronyms, and trying to follow the money can require some thought. But here was one that required almost no thought. It was slam-dunk evidence that "Catholic" Relief Services was doing little else besides lip service to the Faith. It confirmed all the previous reports from those far-off lands that when it comes to the Faith, *those* "Catholic" concerns are near the bottom of the list.

And they *detest* being exposed like this, which is why they go nuclear every time it comes more and more into focus. And this "gay married vice president stationed at headquarters" story really brings it into focus. To show just how un-Catholic "Catholic" Relief Services is, all you have to do is look at the language and sentence construction in their statement in response to the scandal.

They first say that Estridge's job was only technical and did not require to be filled by a Catholic. That's a canard; no one said it *had* to be a Catholic. But at CRS's own headquarters, it should be expected that someone living an intrinsically evil lifestyle would not be employed. To use an example, would CRS allow an out-and-proud racist to occupy a "purely technical" position?

The non-profit characterized our reporting as "attacks" (not realizing that that claim is itself an "attack"). It also broke another sacrosanct rule among liberals by judging. It refers to Estridge as a "child of God." Our question: How do you know the state of his soul? If he's an active homosexual—which all the facts indicate—he's in a state of mortal sin. And if he's in a state of mortal sin, his soul is in serious danger of eternal damnation. This is all fundamental Catholic dogma—but does "Catholic" Relief Services acknowledge that and agree?

And for the theological record, unless Estridge and his sodomite partner are baptized, then they are *not* in fact children of God. Only the baptized are children of the Father. That may come as a shock to their universalist, indifferentist ears at CRS, but that's Church teaching. If CRS doesn't grasp this point, that confirms even more the lack of actual Catholic identity at the non-profit.

Another point: They refer to Mr. Estridge and his sodomy-centered relationship as "a family." Newsflash: Homosexuality-centered relationships *never* constitute a family by definition. They are relationships centered on a sexual practice that is neither life-giving nor life-affirming. That act does not even rise to the level of true sex, as in intercourse. It is nothing more than mutually masturbatory. In no way does a relationship centered on such acts constitute a "family" regardless of whatever emotions may be involved. Best friends don't have to engage in sodomy to show their love and concern for each other.

But herein lies the revelation of the lack of any Catholic identity at CRS. They are theologically bereft. They have misunderstood and misapplied beautiful Catholic social doctrine and cooperated with evil in the process. They hide behind the skirts of the bishops' conference, many of whose members themselves are void of and lacking in solid Catholic formation.

Estridge resigned, more than likely with a handsome wad of cash—cash, by the way, that faithful Catholics in the pews were asked to dig into their pockets and cough up. But don't think he is gone. There is a line in the CRS statement that indicates Estridge may yet reappear in the role of a contract consultant. And in the last paragraph there is whopper: "We are resolute in our commitment to the Church and all its teachings."

They are resolute in their commitment to the Church and all its teachings—all except the one about the intrinsic evil of homosexual acts. We ask: With all your globetrotting for the physically impoverished, did anyone on staff try to convert Mr. Estridge and show him the poverty of his own lifestyle and try to bring him to the truth of Our Blessed Lord and His Holy Catholic Church?

Did any of his superiors show concern at all for the potential scandal caused to the souls of *other* workers in his orbit, who may have had their own faith weakened or even lost owing to this situation? They shouldn't dare claim to be Catholic when they allow a situation within their control to threaten the eternal lives of their staff. They're hypocrites. They run a business largely dependent on government hand-outs and collecting donations from gullible Catholics they like to keep ignorant.

Venerable Abp. Fulton J. Sheen said it best many years ago: The Catholic social justice movement has Judas as its patron saint.

Beware of this outfit, Catholics. Give them nothing of your money. Stop feeding the beast.

Conservative Betrayal
Originally aired June 30, 2015

I F IT'S NOT CATHOLIC, it's pretty much worthless. That's true of just about everything you can think of: education, certainly theology, as well as politics.

In America, too many faithful Catholics—believing, Mass-attending, solid Catholics—are too quick to align themselves with so-called conservative political parties or politicians. It's somewhat understandable that ever since the Democrats aligned themselves with the Culture of Death, faithful Catholics would desert them and go to the only other party with any clout: the GOP. It wasn't surprising to find a large number of Catholics inside the Tea Party as well. Faithful Catholics tune in to Fox News, listen to Rush Limbaugh and feed the conservative political cottage industry of internet personalities like Alex Jones and Glenn Beck.

But our warning holds across the entire spectrum: If it isn't Catholic, watch out.

Faithful, unapologetic, take-no-prisoners, rock-solid Catholic is the only route. Anything else, sooner or later, will betray the truth. Take, for example, Glenn Beck, a former Catholic who is now Mormon. On one of his internet shows in spring 2015, the topic was same-sex "marriage."

"Let me take the pro-gay marriage people and the religious people," Beck commented. "I believe that there is a connecting dot there that nobody is looking at, and that's the Constitution. The question is not whether gay people should be married or not. The question is why is the government involved in our marriage?"

He went on to claim that gay marriage does not "pick my pocket nor break my leg" and therefore the government need not be involved in regulating it. The only time Christians should object is if the government forces them to change their beliefs.

"The agenda is to shut down my freedom of speech and my

belief in—what you don't believe in but I do deeply—the Bible," he explained. "So I'm going to live my life the way I believe. That's freedom of conscience."

He then exhorted his audience to embrace a big-tent approach. "What we need to do, I think, as people who believe in the Constitution, is to start looking for allies who believe in the Constitution and expand our own horizon," he commented. "We would have the ultimate big tent."

No Catholic can support that position. Period.

It's a classic political relativistic "I have my truth; you have your truth" approach that denies objective evil, and reduces morality to personal opinion. He's not arguing for or against morality; he's arguing ultimately for the State to ensure that morality be decided by the individual and then not forced on others.

That's sheer stupidity. There is no such thing as "private" morality. Morality, by its very nature, always, one way or another, involves other people, thereby making it public. The Catholic view of what he said is this: *I support two men or women committing the sin of unnatural sex as long as I'm not forced to accept it by the government.*

This is a classic case of error not having any rights. And it's exactly where many U.S. Catholic leaders went off track decades ago and still remain off track. They say we live in a pluralistic society and cannot impose our beliefs on others. Here's a clue for you: What this Court does is impose the secular view on you. Someone's view is going to be imposed, but Catholic bishops have played footsie with the culture so long because they want to be accepted that they have been blindsided by the speed with which the culture has enslaved them and their sheep. And the view of Glenn Beck is exactly what the bishops are supporting, whether they realize it or not.

They have approached the culture from a "live and let live" ideal. When worldviews are clashing, that never happens. Instead of live and let live, they should be adopting the approach of: *This town ain't big enough for both us.*

Political "conservatives" like Beck and theological "conservatives" like many U.S. bishops have simply accepted the philosophical presumptions of the Culture of Death without making necessary distinctions. There is, for example, an enormous distinction to be made between a case of discrimination and justified discrimination. That's why we have prisons, for example. Murderers and thieves and con artists are justifiably discriminated against because they pose a threat. Marriage between same-sex couples has been justifiably discriminated against because it poses a threat—more than a threat, actually, a danger—to others.

For decades now, Catholics have been betrayed by supposedly conservative bishops and priests, and things are the same in the political world. Just because someone may not hold as horrible a position as the other guy does not make him good or worthy of being heeded. The only voice to be considered is that of Holy Mother the Church. All the rest are wrong. That's why we are here today, at this time in history, chronicling the demise of Western civilization.

If it's not Catholic, it's pretty much worthless.

Clear-Cut Catholicism
Originally aired December 10, 2015

ALL THE MYSTERIES OF CATHOLICISM should be rele-gated to the realm of the divine, things like the Incarnation, the Immaculate Conception, the inner life of the Blessed Trinity, and so forth. The manner in which the teachings of the Church are presented, however, should never be wrapped in mystery.

Yet the modernists and progressives and freemasonic influ-ence within the Church have made a cottage industry of confusing the faithful, making the simplest points so clouded in confusion that Catholics don't understand the Faith. They have, in point of fact, wiped out the idea of objectivity and made just about everything relative.

The black and white of the Faith, the simple yes or no, up or down, on or off of the Faith, has been replaced with murky, fudgy, mealy-mouthed, mushy, compromised vocabulary that in the end can be translated into: "Make up your own mind." It is a monumental betrayal of the Faith and the sheep, and as such is a grave insult to Almighty God.

This is why Church Militant is all about clarity—unam-biguous, straight-up-or-down, objective vocabulary. You will never walk away from our site or our programs wondering where we stand or what we mean—just as it's supposed to be. Our Blessed Lord never left His followers confused. They may not have grasped the fullness of what He said at a given moment or circumstance, but therein lies the mystery of a divine revelation. But He made sure they understood sufficiently before He sent them out into the world to convert it. Yes, clarity, precision, exactness is exactly what the Faith is about.

The mind was created by God for these things. We are hard-wired to receive the truth. Of course, how a given individual responds to it is a different issue, but that in no way excuses leaders from saying things clearly. One of the reasons we at

Church Militant receive such scorn is because we say things clearly and unambiguously. Current conditions in the world don't really allow for that kind of plain speech. We don't care.

Too many are concerned that things be said in such a way that the first and sometimes only consideration is that people's feelings aren't hurt. Of course, no one should make his aim to hurt someone's feelings. One should always act with charity and prudence. But if it comes down to saying something that's true, and the only way it can be said and needs to be said is going to offend someone, then oh well. Better that the truth be told than scandal be borne. True charity demands it.